In the Year1966

by

Kerry Butters.

In the year 1966.

Millennium: 2nd millennium

Centuries: 19th century – **20th century** – 21st century

Decades: 1930s 1940s 1950s – **1960s** – 1970s 1980s 1990s

Years: 1963 1964 1965 – **1966** – 1967 1968 1969

1966 (MCMLXVI) was a common year starting on Saturday (dominical letter B) of the Gregorian calendar, the 1966th year of the Common Era (CE) and *Anno Domini* (AD) designations, the 966th year of the 2nd millennium, the 66th year of the 20th century, and the 7th year of the 1960s decade.

1966 in other calendars

Gregorian calendar	1966 *MCMLXVI*
Ab urbe condita	2719
Armenian calendar	1415 ԹՎ ՌՆԺԵ

Assyrian calendar	6716
Bahá'í calendar	122–123
Bengali calendar	1373
Berber calendar	2916
British Regnal year	14 Eliz. 2 – 15 Eliz. 2
Buddhist calendar	2510
Burmese calendar	1328
Byzantine calendar	7474–7475
Chinese calendar	乙巳年 (Wood Snake) 4662 or 4602 — *to* — 丙午年 (Fire Horse) 4663 or 4603
Coptic calendar	1682–1683

Discordian calendar	3132
Ethiopian calendar	1958–1959
Hebrew calendar	5726–5727
Hindu calendars	
- Vikram Samvat	2022–2023
- Shaka Samvat	1888–1889
- Kali Yuga	5067–5068
Holocene calendar	11966
Igbo calendar	966–967
Iranian calendar	1344–1345
Islamic calendar	1385–1386
Japanese	Shōwa 41

calendar	(昭和４１年)
Juche calendar	55
Julian calendar	Gregorian minus 13 days
Korean calendar	4299
Minguo calendar	ROC 55 民國55年
Thai solar calendar	2509

Contents

Events

January

- January 1 – In a coup, Colonel Jean-Bédel Bokassa takes over as military ruler of the Central African Republic, ousting President David Dacko.
- January 2 – A strike of public transportation workers in New York City begins (it would end January 13).
- January 3 – The first Acid Test is conducted at the Fillmore, San Jose.
- January 4
  - A military coup occurs in Upper Volta (later Burkina Faso).
  - The prime ministers of India and Pakistan meet in Moscow.
  - A gas leak fire at the Feyzin oil refinery near Lyon, France, kills 18 and injures 84.
- January 10
  - Pakistani–Indian peace negotiations end successfully in Tashkent. Indian prime minister Lal Bahadur Shastri dies the next day.

- The French paper *L'Express* publishes a story by Georges Figon, who took part in the kidnapping of Mehdi Ben Barka.
- Georgia House of Representatives refuses to seat Julian Bond.
- Home of civil rights activist Vernon Dahmer in Hattiesburg, Mississippi, is firebombed. Dahmer's family escapes but he dies the next day from severe burns. (White Knights of the Ku Klux Klan Imperial Wizard Samuel Bowers will be unsuccessfully tried for this murder on four occasions, and then convicted in 1998.)
- Commonwealth Prime Ministers' Conference convenes in Lagos, Nigeria.
- January 11
  - A conference on Rhodesia begins in Lagos, Nigeria.
  - The first SR-71 Blackbird spy plane goes into service at Beale AFB.
- January 12 – United States President Lyndon Johnson states that the United States should stay in South Vietnam until Communist aggression there is ended.
- January 13 – Robert C. Weaver becomes the first African-American Cabinet member, by being appointed United States Secretary of Housing and Urban Development.
- January 15 – A bloody military coup is staged in Nigeria, deposing the civilian government.
- January 17
  - The Nigerian coup is overturned by another faction of the military, leaving a military government in power. This is the beginning of a long period of military rule.

- A B-52 bomber collides with a KC-135 Stratotanker over Spain, dropping three 70-kiloton hydrogen bombs near the town of Palomares, and one into the sea, in the 1966 Palomares B-52 crash.
- Carl Brashear, the first African-American United States Navy diver, is involved in an accident during the recovery of a lost H-bomb which results in the amputation of his leg.
- January 18
  - French police announce that Georges Figon has committed suicide, prior to his arrest for the kidnapping of Mehdi Ben Barka.
  - About 8,000 U.S. soldiers land in South Vietnam; U.S. troops now total 190,000.
- January 19 – Indira Gandhi is elected Prime Minister of India; she is sworn in January 24.
- January 20 – Demonstrations occur against high food prices in Hungary.
- January 21 – Italian Prime Minister Aldo Moro resigns due to a power struggle in his party.
- January 22
  - The military government of Nigeria announces that ex-prime minister Abubakar Tafawa Balewa was killed during the coup.
  - The Chadian Muslim insurgent group FROLINAT is founded in Sudan, starting the Chadian Civil War.
- January 24 – Air India Flight 101 crashes into Mont Blanc, killing all 117 persons on board, including Dr. Homi J. Bhabha, chairman of the Indian Atomic Energy Commission.
- January 26

- o Harold Holt becomes Prime Minister of Australia when Robert Menzies retires.
- o Beaumont children disappearance: Three children disappear on their way to Glenelg, South Australia, never to be seen again.
- January 27
  - o The British government promises the U.S. that British troops in Malaysia will stay until more peaceful conditions occur in the region.
  - o Britain's Labour Party unexpectedly retains the parliamentary seat of Hull North in a by-election, with a swing of 4.5% to their candidate from the opposition Conservatives, and a majority up from 1,181 at the 1964 General Election to 5,351.
- January 29 – The first of 608 performances of *Sweet Charity* opens at the Palace Theatre in New York City.
- January 31 – The United Kingdom ceases all trade with Rhodesia.

February

- February 1 – West Germany procures some 2,600 political prisoners from East Germany.
- February 3 – The unmanned Soviet Luna 9 spacecraft makes the first controlled rocket-assisted landing on the Moon.
- February 4 – All Nippon Airways Flight 60 plunges into Tokyo Bay; 133 are killed.
- February 6 – The TV series *Mister Ed* airs its final episode (ran 1961–66).

- February 7 – Lyndon Johnson of the United States and Nguyễn Cao Kỳ of South Vietnam convene with other officials in Honolulu, Hawaii to discuss the course of the Vietnam War.
- February 8 – The National Hockey League announces it will expand to 12 teams for the 1967 season.
- February 10 – Soviet writers Yuli Daniel and Andrei Sinyavsky are sentenced to five and seven years, respectively, for "anti-Soviet" writings.
- February 12 – Vietnam War: The Tây Vinh Massacre occurs.
- February 14 – The Australian dollar is introduced at a rate of 2 dollars per pound, or 10 shillings per dollar.
- February 19 – The naval minister of the United Kingdom, Christopher Mayhew, resigns.
- February 20 – While Soviet author and translator Valery Tarsis is abroad, the Soviet Union negates his citizenship.
- February 23 – An intra-party military coup d'état in Syria replaces the previous government of Amin al-Hafiz by one led by Salah Jadid.
- February 24 – A coup d'état led by the police and military of Ghana raises the National Liberation Council to power while president Kwame Nkrumah is abroad.
- February 26
  - Gò Dài massacre: Vietnam War.
  - A curfew is declared in Jakarta, Indonesia.
- February 28
  - British Prime Minister Harold Wilson calls a General Election in the United Kingdom, to be held on 31 March.

- U.S. astronauts Charles Bassett and Elliot See are killed in an aircraft accident in St. Louis, Missouri.

March

- March – The DKW automobile ceases production in Germany.
- March 1
  - The British Government announces plans for the decimalisation of the pound sterling (hitherto denominated in 20 shillings and 240 pence to the £), to come into force in February 1971 (Decimal Day).
  - Soviet space probe *Venera 3* crashes on Venus, becoming the first spacecraft to land on another planet's surface.
  - The Ba'ath Party takes power in Syria.
  - The Frost Report, which launched the television careers of John Cleese, Ronnie Barker and Ronnie Corbett and also the careers of other writers and performers, is first broadcast on BBC.
- March 2 – Kwame Nkrumah arrives in Guinea and is granted asylum.
- March 4
  - Canadian Pacific Air Lines Flight 402 crashes during a night landing in poor visibility at Tokyo International Airport in Japan, killing 64 of 72 persons on board.
  - In an interview with *London Evening Standard* reporter Maureen Cleave, John Lennon of The Beatles states that they are "more popular than Jesus now".
- March 5

- BOAC Flight 911 crashes in severe clear-air turbulence over Mount Fuji soon after taking off from Tokyo International Airport in Japan, killing all 124 people on board.
- A massive theft of nuclear materials is revealed in Brazil.
- *Merci, Chérie* by Udo Jürgens (music by Udo Jürgens, lyrics by Udo Jürgens and Thomas Hörbiger) wins the Eurovision Song Contest 1966 for Austria.
- March 7 – Charles de Gaulle asks U.S. President Lyndon B. Johnson for negotiations about the state of NATO equipment in France.
- March 8
  - Anti-communist demonstrations occur at the Indonesian Foreign Ministry.
  - Vietnam War: The U.S. announces it will substantially increase the number of its troops in Vietnam.
  - Nelson's Pillar in O'Connell Street, Dublin, is clandestinely blown up by former Irish Republican Army volunteers marking this year's 50th anniversary of the Easter Rising.
- March 9 – Ronnie, one of the Kray twins, shoots George Cornell (an associate of rivals The Richardson Gang) dead at The Blind Beggar pub in Whitechapel, east London, a crime for which he is finally convicted in 1969.
- March 10 – Crown Princess Beatrix of the Netherlands marries Claus von Amsberg. Some spectators demonstrate against the groom because he is German.
- March 11

- Transition to the New Order in Indonesia: President Sukarno gives all executive powers to General Suharto by signing the "Supersemar" order.
  - French President Charles de Gaulle states that French troops will be taken out of NATO and that all French NATO bases and HQ's must be closed within a year.
- March 12 – Bobby Hull of the Chicago Blackhawks sets the National Hockey League single season scoring record against the New York Rangers with his 51st goal.
- March 16 – NASA spacecraft *Gemini 8* (David Scott, Neil Armstrong) conducts the first docking in space, with an Agena target vehicle.
- Paul Van Doren established the Vans shoe company in California.
- March 17
  - More anti-communist demonstrations occur in Indonesia.
  - Off the Mediterranean coast of Spain, the United States Navy submersible DSV *Alvin* finds a missing U.S. hydrogen bomb.
- March 19 – The Texas Western Miners defeat the Kentucky Wildcats with five African-American starters, ushering in desegregation in athletic recruiting.
- March 20 – Football's Jules Rimet Trophy is stolen while on exhibition in London; it is found seven days later by a mongrel dog named "Pickles" and his owner David Corbett, wrapped in newspaper in a south London garden.
- March 22 – In Washington, D.C., General Motors President James M. Roche appears before a Senate subcommittee, and apologizes to consumer advocate Ralph Nader for the

company's intimidation and harassment campaign against him.

- March 23 – Pope Paul VI and Michael Ramsey, the Archbishop of Canterbury, meet in Rome.
- March 26 – Demonstrations are held across the United States against the Vietnam War.
- March 27 – In South Vietnam, 20,000 Buddhists march in demonstrations against the policies of the military government.
- March 28
  - Cevdet Sunay becomes the fifth president of Turkey.
  - Indira Gandhi visits Washington, D.C.
- March 29 – The 23rd Communist Party Conference is held in the Soviet Union; Leonid Brezhnev demands that U.S. troops leave Vietnam, and announces that Chinese-Soviet relations are not satisfactory.
- March 31
  - The British Labour Party led by Harold Wilson wins the United Kingdom General Election, gaining a 96-seat majority (compared with a single seat majority when the election was called on February 28).
  - The Soviet Union launches *Luna 10*, which later becomes the first space probe to enter orbit around the Moon.

April

- April 2 – The Indonesian army demands that the country rejoin the United Nations.

- April 3 – *Luna 10* is the first manmade object to enter lunar orbit.
- April 7 – The United Kingdom asks the United Nations Security Council for authority to use force to stop oil tankers that violate the embargo against Rhodesia (authority is given April 10).
- April 8
    - Buddhists in South Vietnam protest against the fact that the new government has not set a date for free elections.
    - Leonid Brezhnev becomes General Secretary of the Soviet Union, as well as Leader of the Communist Party of the U.S.S.R.
    - *Time* magazine cover story asks "Is God Dead?"
- April 9 – The captain of English football league club Norwich City F.C., Barry Butler, is killed in a car accident.
- April 13
    - United States' magazine *Time*'s cover story is 'London: The Swinging City'
    - United States president Lyndon Johnson signs the 1966 Uniform Time Act, dealing with daylight saving time.
- April 14
    - Kenyan Vice President Oginga Odinga resigns, saying "invisible government" representing foreign interests now runs the country. Will head a new party, the Kenya People's Union.
    - The South Vietnamese government promises free elections in 3–5 months.
- April 15 – An anti-Nasser conspiracy is exposed in Egypt.
- April 18

- China declares that it will stop economic aid to Indonesia.
  - The 38th Academy Awards ceremony is held.
- April 19 – Bobbi Gibb becomes the first woman to run the Boston Marathon.
- April 21
  - An artificial heart is installed in the chest of Marcel DeRudder in a Houston, Texas hospital.
  - The opening of the Parliament of the United Kingdom is televised for the first time.
  - Haile Selassie visits Jamaica for the first time, meeting with Rasta leaders.
  - Ian Brady and Myra Hindley go on trial at Chester Crown Court, for the murders of 3 children who vanished between November 1963 and October 1965.
- April 24 – Uniform daylight saving time is first observed in most parts of North America.
- April 26
  - A new government is formed in the Republic of the Congo, led by Ambroise Noumazalaye.
  - The magnitude 5.1 Tashkent earthquake affects the largest city in Soviet Central Asia with a maximum MSK intensity of VII (*Very strong*). Tashkent is mostly destroyed and 15–200 are killed.
- April 27 – Pope Paul VI and Soviet Foreign Minister Andrei Gromyko meet in the Vatican (the first meeting between leaders of the Roman Catholic Church and the Soviet Union).
- April 28 – In Rhodesia, security forces kill seven ZANLA men in combat; *Chimurenga*, the ZANU rebellion, begins.

- April 29 – U.S. troops in Vietnam total 250,000.
- April 30
  - Regular hovercraft service begins over the English Channel (discontinued in 2000 due to the Channel Tunnel).
  - The Church of Satan is formed by Anton Szandor LaVey in San Francisco.

May

- May 1 – Floods occur on the Finnish coast.
- May 3 – Swinging Radio England and Britain Radio commence broadcasting on AM, with a combined potential 100,000 watts, from the same ship anchored off the south coast of England in international waters.
- May 4 – Fiat signs a contract with the Soviet government to build a car factory in the Soviet Union.
- May 5 – The Montreal Canadiens defeat the Detroit Red Wings to win the Stanley Cup.
- May 6 – The Moors murders trial ends with Ian Brady being found guilty on all three counts of murder and sentenced to three concurrent terms of life imprisonment. Myra Hindley is convicted on two counts of murder and of being an accessory in the third murder committed by Brady, and receives two concurrent terms of life imprisonment and a seven-year fixed term for being an accessory.
- The hit song "Paint It Black" by the Rolling Stones was released
- May 7 – Irish bank workers go on strike.
- May 12

- African members of the UN Security Council say that the British army should blockade Rhodesia.
- The Busch Memorial Stadium opens in St Louis, Missouri.
- Radio Peking claims that U.S. planes have shot down a Chinese plane over Yunnan (the U.S. denies the story the next day).
- May 14 – Turkey and Greece intend to start negotiations about the situation in Cyprus.
- May 15
  - Indonesia asks Malaysia for peace negotiations.
  - The South Vietnamese army besieges Da Nang.
  - Tens of thousands of anti-war demonstrators again picket the White House, then rally at the Washington Monument.
- May 16
  - The Communist Party of China issues the 'May 16 Notice', marking the beginning of the Cultural Revolution.
  - A seamen's strike is called in Britain.
  - The legendary album *Pet Sounds* by The Beach Boys is released.
  - Bob Dylan's seminal album, *Blonde on Blonde* is released in the U.S.
  - In New York City, Dr. Martin Luther King Jr. makes his first public speech on the Vietnam War.
- May 19 – Gertrude Baniszewski is found guilty of murdering and torturing Sylvia Likens and is sentenced to life in prison (she is released on parole in December 1985).
- May 24

- ◦ Battle of Mengo Hill: Ugandan army troops arrest Mutesa II of Buganda and occupy his palace.
  - ◦ The Nigerian government forbids all political activity in the country until January 17, 1969.
- May 25 – Explorer program: *Explorer 32* is launched.
  - ◦ No. 9 Squadron RAAF becomes part of the 4,500 strong Australian Task Force assigned to duties in Vietnam, leaving for Southeast Asia aboard the aircraft carrier HMAS *Sydney*.
- May 26 – Guyana achieves independence.
- May 28
  - ◦ *It's a Small World* opens at Disneyland.
  - ◦ Fidel Castro declares martial law in Cuba because of a possible U.S. attack.
  - ◦ The Indonesian and Malaysian governments declare that the Indonesia–Malaysia confrontation is over (a treaty is signed on August 11).
- May 31 – The Philippines reestablishes diplomatic relations with Malaysia.

June

- June 1
  - ◦ The final new episode of *The Dick Van Dyke Show* airs (the first episode aired on October 3, 1961).
  - ◦ White House Conference on Civil Rights
- June 2
  - ◦ Éamon de Valera is re-elected as Irish president.

- Surveyor program: *Surveyor 1* lands in Oceanus Procellarum on the Moon, becoming the first U.S. spacecraft to soft-land on another world.
  - Four former cabinet ministers including Évariste Kimba are executed in the Democratic Republic of the Congo, for alleged involvement in a plot to kill Mobutu Sese Seko.
- June 3 – Joaquín Balaguer is elected president of the Dominican Republic.
- June 5 – *Gemini 9*: Gene Cernan completes the second U.S. spacewalk (2 hours, 7 minutes).
- June 6 – Civil rights activist James Meredith is shot while traversing Mississippi in the March Against Fear.
- June 8
  - An XB-70 Valkyrie prototype is destroyed in a mid-air collision with a F-104 Starfighter chase plane during a photo shoot. NASA pilot Joseph A. Walker and USAF test pilot Carl Cross are both killed.
  - Topeka, Kansas is devastated by a tornado that registers as an "F5" on the Fujita scale, the first to exceed US $100 million in damages. Sixteen people are killed, hundreds more injured, and thousands of homes damaged or destroyed, and the campus of Washburn University suffers catastrophic damage.
- June 12 – Chicago's Division Street riots begin, in response to police shooting of a young Puerto Rican man.
- June 13 – *Miranda v. Arizona*: The Supreme Court of the United States rules that the police must inform suspects of their rights before questioning them.

- June 14 – The Vatican abolishes the *Index Librorum Prohibitorum* (index of banned books).
- June 17 – An Air France personnel strike begins.
- June 18 – CIA chief William Raborn resigns; Richard Helms becomes his successor.
- June 20 – French President Charles de Gaulle starts his visit to the Soviet Union.
- June 21 – Opposition leader Arthur Calwell is shot after attending a political meeting in Mosman, Sydney, Australia.
- June 27
  - Frank Zappa and The Mothers of Invention's debut album, *Freak Out!*, is released. It is an initial failure, but gains a massive cult following in subsequent years.
  - The gothic soap opera *Dark Shadows* premieres on ABC.
- June 28 – In Argentina, a junta calling itself *Revolución Argentina* deposes president Arturo Umberto Illia in a coup, and appoints General Juan Carlos Onganía to lead.
- June 29
  - Juan Carlos Onganía comes to power in "Argentine Revolution" coup d'état.
  - A sailors' strike, organised by the National Union of Seamen, ends in the United Kingdom.
  - Vietnam War: U.S. planes begin bombing Hanoi and Haiphong.
- June 30
  - France formally leaves NATO.
  - The National Organization for Women (NOW) is founded in Washington, D.C.

July

- July – Gangster Charlie Richardson is arrested by police and sentenced to 25 years in prison in the following year for his part in the Torture Gang assaults.
- July 1 – Joaquín Balaguer becomes president of the Dominican Republic.
- July 3
  - 31 people are arrested when a demonstration by approximately 4,000 anti-Vietnam War protesters in front of the U.S. Embassy in London's Grosvenor Square turns violent
  - René Barrientos is elected president of Bolivia.
- July 4
  - North Vietnam declares general mobilization.
  - American President Lyndon B. Johnson signs the Freedom of Information Act, which goes into effect the following year.
  - Congress of Racial Equality (CORE) endorses goal of Black Power at well attended convention in Baltimore. Martin Luther King, Jr., and Roy Wilkins criticize this declaration.
- July 6 – Malawi becomes a republic.
- July 7 – A Warsaw Pact conference ends with a promise to support North Vietnam.
- July 8 – King Mwambutsa IV Bangiriceng of Burundi is deposed by his son Ntare V, who is in turn deposed by prime minister Michel Micombero.
- July 11
  - The 1966 FIFA World Cup begins in England.

- British Motor Corporation and Jaguar Cars announce plans to merge as British Motor Holdings.
- July 12
  - Indira Gandhi visits Moscow.
  - Zambia threatens to leave the Commonwealth of Nations because of British peace overtures to Rhodesia.
- July 13 – The International Society for Krishna Consciousness is founded in New York City by A. C. Bhaktivedanta Swami Prabhupada.
- July 14
  - Israeli and Syrian jet fighters clash over the Jordan River.
  - Richard Speck murders 8 student nurses in their Chicago dormitory. He is arrested on July 17.
  - Gwynfor Evans, President of Plaid Cymru, becomes Member of the United Kingdom Parliament for Carmarthen, taking the previously Labour-held Welsh seat at a by-election with a majority of 2,435 on an 18% swing, and giving Plaid Cymru its first representation at Westminster in its forty-one year history.
- July 16 – British Prime Minister Harold Wilson flies to Moscow to try to start peace negotiations about the Vietnam War (the Soviet government rejects his ideas).
- July 18
  - *Gemini 10* (John Young, Michael Collins) is launched. After docking with an Agena target vehicle, the astronauts then set a world altitude record of 474 miles (763 km).
  - The Hough Riots break out in Cleveland, Ohio, the city's first race riot.

- Australian children's television series Play School airs for the first time, going on to become the longest-running children's show in Australia, and the second longest running children's show in the world.
- July 22 – The Chinese government declares Dutch delegate G. J. Jongejans persona non grata, but tells him not to leave the country before a group of Chinese engineers has left the Netherlands.
- July 23 – Katangese troops in Stanleyville, Congo, revolt for several weeks in support of the exiled minister Moise Tshombe.
- July 24 – U.N. Secretary General U Thant visits Moscow.
- July 26 – Lord Gardiner issues the Practice Statement in the House of Lords, stating that the House is not bound to follow its own previous precedent.
- July 28 – The U.S. announces that a Lockheed U-2 reconnaissance plane has disappeared over Cuba.
- July 29
  - A military counter-coup in Nigeria: army officers from the north of the country execute head of state General Aguiyi-Ironsi an install Yakubu Gowon.
  - *La Noche de los Bastones Largos*: Junta takes over Argentine universities.
  - Bob Dylan is injured in a motorcycle accident near his home in Woodstock, New York. He is not seen in public for over a year.
- July 30 – England beats West Germany 4–2 to win the 1966 FIFA World Cup at Wembley after extra time.

August

- August 1
  - Sniper Charles Whitman kills 14 people and wounds 32 from atop the University of Texas at Austin Main Building tower, after earlier killing his wife and mother.
  - British Colonial Office merges with Commonwealth Relations Office to form new Commonwealth Office.
- August 2 – The Spanish government forbids overflights of British military aircraft.
- August 5
  - Groundbreaking takes place for the World Trade Center.
  - Martin Luther King Jr. leads a civil rights march in Chicago, during which he is struck by a rock thrown from an angry white mob.
  - The Caesars Palace hotel and casino opens in Las Vegas.
  - The Beatles' *Revolver* LP is released in the United Kingdom.
- August 6
  - Braniff Flight 250 crashes in Falls City, Nebraska, killing all 42 on board.
  - René Barrientos takes office as the president of Bolivia.
  - The Salazar Bridge (now the 25 de Abril Bridge) opens in Lisbon, Portugal.
- August 7 – Race riots occur in Lansing, Michigan.
- August 10

- An East German court sentences Günter Laudahn to life imprisonment for spying for the United States.
  - Lunar Orbiter 1, the first U.S. spacecraft to orbit the moon, is launched.
- August 11 –
  - Indonesia and Malaysia issue joint peace declaration, formally ending the Indonesia–Malaysia confrontation which began in 1963.
  - The Beatles hold a press conference in Chicago, during which John Lennon apologizes for his "more popular than Jesus" remark, saying, "I didn't mean it as a lousy anti-religious thing."
- August 12 – Massacre of Braybrook Street: Harry Roberts, John Duddy and Jack Witney shoot dead 3 plainclothes policemen in London; they are later sentenced to life imprisonment.
- August 13
  - In the People's Republic of China, Mao Zedong begins the Cultural Revolution to purge and reorganize China's Communist Party.
  - An earthquake in Varto town, Turkey, kills 2,394 and injures 10,000.
- August 15
  - Syrian and Israeli troops clash over Lake Kinneret (also known as the Sea of Galilee) for 3 hours.
  - It is announced that the *New York Herald Tribune* will not resume publication.
- August 16 – Vietnam War: The House Un-American Activities Committee starts investigating Americans who have aided the Viet Cong, with the intent to make these

activities illegal. Anti-war demonstrators disrupt the meeting and 50 are arrested.

- August 17 – Saudi Arabia and the United Arab Republic begin negotiations in Kuwait to end the war in Yemen.
- August 18 – Vietnam War – Battle of Long Tan: D Company, 6th Battalion of the Royal Australian Regiment, meets and defeats a Viet Cong force estimated to be four times larger, in Phuoc Tuy Province, Republic of Vietnam.
- August 19 – An earthquake in eastern Turkey destroys whole cities.
- August 21 – Seven men are sentenced to death in Egypt, for anti-Nasser agitation.
- August 22
  - The Asian Development Bank (ADB) established.
  - The United Farm Workers Organizing Committee (UFWOC), predecessor of the United Farm Workers of America (UFW), is formed.
- August 24 – The Doors record their self-titled debut LP.
- August 26
  - Riots occur in French Somaliland.
  - The first battle of the South African Air Force and the South African Police with PLAN, the armed wing of the South West Africa People's Organization (SWAPO), takes place at Ongulumbashe in Northern South West Africa during Operation Blue Wildebeest. This battle starts the South African Border War which continues until 1989.
- August 29 – The Beatles end their US tour with a concert at Candlestick Park in San Francisco. It is their last performance as a live touring band.

- August 30 – France offers independence to French Somaliland (later Djibouti in 1977).

September

- September 1
  - United Nations Secretary-General U Thant declares that he will not seek re-election, because U.N. efforts in Vietnam have failed.
  - 98 British tourists die in an air crash in Ljubljana, Yugoslavia.
  - While waiting at a bus stop Ralph Baer, an inventor with Sanders Associates, writes a four-page document that lays out the basic principles for creating a video game to be played on a television: the beginning of a multibillion-dollar industry.
- September 6 – In Cape Town, South Africa, the architect of Apartheid, Prime Minister Hendrik Verwoerd, is stabbed to death by Dimitri Tsafendas during a parliamentary meeting.
- September 7 – The ocean liner SS *Hanseatic* catches fire and burns in New York Harbor.
- September 8 – *Star Trek*, the science fiction television series, debuts on NBC-TV in the United States with its first episode, titled "The Man Trap".
- September 9 – NATO decides to move SHAPE headquarters to Belgium.
- September 12 The Monkees premiere on NBC
  - *Gemini 11* (Richard F. Gordon, Jr., Pete Conrad) docks with an Agena target vehicle.

- B. J. Vorster becomes the new Prime Minister of South Africa.
- September 13 – Clashes between the Chinese Communist Party and the Red Guards are reported by TASS in the Soviet Union.
- September 16
  - In South Vietnam, Thích Trí Quang ends a 100-day hunger strike.
  - The Metropolitan Opera House opens at Lincoln Center in New York City with the world premiere of Samuel Barber's opera *Antony and Cleopatra*.
- September 18 – Valerie Percy, 21-year-old daughter of U.S. Senate candidate Charles H. Percy, is stabbed and bludgeoned to death in the family mansion on Chicago's North Shore.
- September 19
  - Scotland Yard arrests Buster Edwards, suspected of involvement in the Great Train Robbery.
  - Timothy Leary forms the spiritual group League for Spiritual Discovery.
  - Indonesian military commander (later President) Suharto announces the resumption of Indonesian participation in the United Nations.
- September 29 – Hurricane Inez strikes Hispaniola, leaving thousands dead and tens of thousands homeless in the Dominican Republic and Haiti.
- September 30
  - The Bechuanaland Protectorate in Africa achieves independence from the United Kingdom as Botswana, with Seretse Khama as its first President.

- Baldur von Schirach and Albert Speer are released from Spandau Prison.

October

- October
  - Bobby Seale and Huey P. Newton found the Black Panther Party.
  - The Toyota Corolla car is introduced.
- October 1 – West Coast Airlines Flight 956 crashes with 18 fatal injuries and no survivors 5.5 miles (8.9 km) south of Wemme, Oregon. This accident marks the first loss of a DC-9.
- October 3 – Tunisia severs diplomatic relations with the United Arab Republic.
- October 4
  - Israel applies for membership in the EEC.
  - Basutoland becomes independent and takes the name Lesotho.
- October 5
  - UNESCO signs the Recommendation Concerning the Status of Teachers. This event is now celebrated as World Teachers' Day.
  - An experimental Reactor at the Enrico Fermi Nuclear Generating Station suffers a partial meltdown when its cooling system fails.
- October 6
  - LSD is made illegal in the United States and controlled so strictly that not only are possession and recreational

use criminalized, but all legal scientific research programs on the drug in the US are shut down as well.
  - The Love Pageant Rally takes place in the Panhandle of Golden Gate Park, a narrower section that projects into San Francisco's Haight-Ashbury district.
- October 7 – The Soviet Union declares that all Chinese students must leave the country before the end of October.
- October 9
  - Vietnam War: Binh Tai Massacre.
  - Vietnam War: Diên Niên - Phước Bình massacre.
- October 11 – France and the Soviet Union sign a treaty for cooperation in nuclear research.
- October 14
  - Closure of Intra Bank begins crisis of Lebanese banking system.
  - The city of Montreal inaugurates its metro system (see Montreal Metro).
- October 15
  - U.S. President Lyndon B. Johnson signs a bill creating the United States Department of Transportation.
  - The U.S. Congress passes a bill for the creation of Pictured Rocks National Lakeshore.
  - ABC-TV telecasts a highly acclaimed 90-minute television adaptation of the musical *Brigadoon*, starring Robert Goulet, Peter Falk, and Sally Ann Howes. It wins many Emmy Awards and inaugurates a short-lived series of special television adaptations of famous Broadway musicals on ABC. Goulet stars in all but one of these specials.

- October 16 – Grace Slick performs live for the first time with Jefferson Airplane.
- October 17 – Lesotho and Botswana are admitted to the United Nations.
- October 21
  - The Aberfan disaster occurs in South Wales, United Kingdom.
  - The AFL-NFL merger is approved by the U.S. Congress.
- October 22
  - British spy George Blake escapes from Wormwood Scrubs prison; he is next seen in Moscow.
  - Spain demands that the United Kingdom stop military flights to Gibraltar; Britain refuses the next day.
- October 24 – Negotiations about the Vietnam War begin in Manila, Philippines.
- October 25
  - A military court in Jakarta sentences ex-foreign minister Subandrio to death.
  - Spain closes its Gibraltar border to non-pedestrian traffic.
- October 26
  - NATO moves its HQ from Paris to Brussels.
  - A fire aboard the aircraft carrier USS *Oriskany* in the Gulf of Tonkin kills 44 crewmen.
- October 27 – The United Nations takes Namibia from South Africa.
- October 29

- The first ever regeneration in *Doctor Who* of the Doctor: William Hartnell's face transforms into that of Patrick Troughton.
- The Guinean delegation to the OAU meeting in Ethiopia, become hostages of the Ghanaian government in Accra.

November

- November 2 – The Cuban Adjustment Act comes into force, allowing 123,000 Cubans the opportunity to apply for permanent residence in the United States.
- November 4 – In Italy, a flood of the Arno River hits Florence, flooding it to a maximum depth of 6.7 m (22 ft), leaving thousands homeless and destroying millions of masterpieces of art and rare books. In addition, a severe tidal flood hits Venice.
- November 5 – Thirty-eight African states demand that the United Kingdom use force against the Rhodesian government.
- November 6 – Lunar Orbiter 2 is launched.
- November 8
  - Former Massachusetts Attorney General Edward Brooke becomes the first African American elected to the United States Senate since Reconstruction.
  - Actor Ronald Reagan is elected Governor of California.
- November 9 – John Lennon meets Yoko Ono at the Indica Gallery, London.

- November 10 – Seán Lemass retires as Taoiseach of the Republic of Ireland to be replaced in the role by fellow Fianna Fáil member Jack Lynch.
- November 11
  - A mine kills 3 Israeli paratroopers on the West Bank border.
  - Spain declares general amnesty for crimes committed during the Spanish Civil War (effective only for the Falangists' side).
- November 14 – Jack L. Warner sells Warner Bros. to Seven Arts Productions, which eventually becomes Warner Bros.-Seven Arts.
- November 15
  - *Gemini 12* (James A. Lovell, Buzz Aldrin), splashes down safely in the Atlantic Ocean, 600 km east of the Bahamas.
  - Harry Maurice Roberts, who killed 3 policemen in August, is caught near London.
  - A Boeing 727 carrying Pan Am Flight 708 crashes near Berlin, Germany, killing all three people on board.
  - Two young couples in Point Pleasant, West Virginia reportedly see a strange moth-like creature better known as the Mothman.
- November 16 – U.S. doctor Sam Sheppard is acquitted in his second trial for the murder of his pregnant wife in 1954.
- November 17
  - The U.N. General Assembly decides to found the United Nations Industrial Development Organization.
  - A spectacular Leonid meteor shower passes over Arizona, at the rate of 2,300 a minute for 20 minutes.

- November 21 – In Togo, the army crushes an attempted coup.
- November 24
  - The Beatles begin recording sessions for their *Sgt. Pepper's Lonely Hearts Club Band* L.P.
  - Bulgarian TABSO Flight 101 crashes near Bratislava, Czechoslovakia, killing all 82 people on board.
- November 26 – The Saskatchewan Roughriders defeat the Ottawa Rough Riders to win the 54th Grey Cup at Vancouver's Empire Stadium 29-14. Saskatchewan were led by quarterback Ron Lancaster.
- November 27 – The Washington Redskins defeat the New York Giants 72–41 in the highest scoring game in NFL history.
- November 28 – Truman Capote's Black and White Ball ('The Party of the Century') is held in New York City.
- November 29 – The SS *Daniel J. Morrell* sinks in a storm on Lake Huron, killing 28 of its 29 crewmen.
- November 30 – Barbados achieves independence.

December

- December 1
  - Kurt Georg Kiesinger is elected Chancellor of West Germany.
  - British Prime Minister Harold Wilson and Rhodesian Prime minister Ian Smith negotiate on the HMS *Tiger* in the Mediterranean.
- December 2 – U Thant agrees to serve a second term as U.N. Secretary General.

- December 3 – Anti-Portuguese demonstrations occur in Macau; a curfew is declared the next day.
- December 5 – U.S. Supreme Court rules in *Bond v. Floyd* that the Georgia House of Representatives must seat Julian Bond, having violated his First and Fourteenth Amendment rights.
- December 6 – Bình Hòa massacre: Vietnam War.
- December 7
  - Syria offers weapons to rebels in Jordan.
  - Barbados is admitted to the United Nations.
- December 8 – The Typaldos Line's ferry SS *Heraklion* sinks in rough seas, in the Aegean Sea near Crete, leaving 217 dead.
- December 15 – Walt Disney dies while producing *The Jungle Book*, the last animated feature under his personal supervision.
- December 16
  - The U.N. Security Council approves an oil embargo against Rhodesia.
  - The International Covenant on Economic, Social and Cultural Rights and the International Covenant on Civil and Political Rights are adopted by the General Assembly, as Resolution 2200 A (XXI).
- December 17 – South Africa does not join the trade embargo against Rhodesia.
- December 18 – *How the Grinch Stole Christmas*, narrated by Boris Karloff, is shown for the first time on CBS, beginning an annual Christmas tradition in the USA.
- December 19 – The Asian Development Bank begins operations.
- December 20 – Harold Wilson withdraws all his previous offers to the Rhodesian government, and announces that he

will agree to independence only after the founding of a Black majority government.

- December 22 – Prime Minister Ian Smith declares that Rhodesia is already a republic.
- December 24 – New York television station WPIX broadcasts its Christmas tradition, "The Yule Log" for the first time.
- December 26 – The first Kwanzaa is celebrated by Maulana Karenga, founder of Organization US (a black nationalist group) and later chair of Black Studies at California State University, Long Beach, from 1989 to 2002.
- December 31
  - East German Premier Walter Ulbricht discusses negotiations about German reunification.
  - Thieves steal millions' worth of paintings from the Dulwich Art Gallery in London.
  - The Congolese government takes over the Union Minière du Haut Katanga.

Date unknown

- Konstantin Chernenko, later leader of the Soviet Union, becomes a candidate member of the Central Committee.
- Paramount Pictures Corporation becomes a wholly owned subsidiary of Gulf+Western Industries, Inc.
- The Surrealist Movement in the United States is founded by Franklin and Penelope Rosemont.
- Lise Meitner and Otto Hahn are awarded the Fermi Prize.
- The Congress of the United States creates the National Council for Marine Resources and Engineering Development.

- Martin Richards designs the programming language BCPL.
- The World Buddhist Sangha Council is convened by Theravadins in Sri Lanka, with the hope of bridging differences and working together.
- *The Jerusalem Bible*, a Roman Catholic translation, is published in English.
- Peter L. Berger and Thomas Luckmann publish *The Social Construction of Reality*.
- Long-term potentiation (LTP), the putative cellular mechanism of learning and memory, is first observed by Terje Lømo in Oslo, Norway.
- In or about this year, one person returning to Haiti from the Congo is thought to have first brought HIV to the Americas.

Births

January

Patrick Dempsey

Lena Philipsson

Romário

- January 1 – Anna Burke, Australian politician
- January 4 – Deana Carter, American singer
- January 5
  - Yuri Amano, Japanese voice actress
  - Kate Schellenbach, American musician
- January 7
  - Carolyn Bessette-Kennedy, American actress and model, wife of John F. Kennedy, Jr. (d. 1999)
  - Ehab Tawfik, Egyptian singer

- January 8 – Igor Vyazmikin, Russian ice hockey player
- January 13 – Patrick Dempsey, American actor
- January 17
    - George Morikawa, Japanese author and illustrator
    - Shabba Ranks, Jamaican singer
    - António Zeferino, Cape Verdean athlete
- January 19
    - Floris Jan Bovelander, Dutch field-hockey player
    - Stefan Edberg, Swedish tennis player
    - Lena Philipsson, Swedish singer and media personality
- January 20 – Rainn Wilson, American actor
- January 22 – Jegath Gaspar Raj, Tamil Maiyam Founder
- January 24 – Jimeoin, Northern Irish-Australian comedian and actor
- January 28
    - Andrea Berg, German singer
    - Seiji Mizushima, Japanese anime director
- January 29 – Romário, Brazilian footballer
- January 30 – Neal Chase, American Exilarch religious educator
- January 30 – Hans Tutschku, German composer
- January 31 – Gordon Hill, British internet celebrity and meme known as The Wealdstone Raider

February

Sean Harris

Sarah Montague

Billy Zane

- February 1 – Michelle Akers, American footballer

- February 4 – Kyōko Koizumi, Japanese actress and singer
- February 5 – José María Olazábal, Spanish golfer
- February 6 – Rick Astley, British rock singer
- February 7 – Kristin Otto, German swimmer
- February 8
  - Sean Harris, English actor
  - Sarah Montague, English journalist and radio host
  - Hristo Stoichkov, Bulgarian footballer
- February 9
  - Christoph Maria Herbst, German actor
  - Ellen van Langen, Dutch athlete
- February 10 – Daryl Johnston, American football player
- February 11 – Stephen Gregory, American actor
- February 13 – Neal McDonough, American actor
- February 16 – Martin Perscheid, German cartoonist
- February 17 – Luc Robitaille, Canadian hockey player
- February 18 – Richard A. Collins, British scientist and author
- February 20 – Cindy Crawford, American model and actress
- February 22
  - Yahya Ayyash, Palestinian bombmaker
  - Rachel Dratch, American actress and comedienne
  - Brian Greig, Australian politician
- February 23 – Michael Arata, American actor
- February 24 – Billy Zane, American actor
- February 25
  - Samson Kitur, Kenyan athlete
  - Téa Leoni, American actress
- February 26 – Najwa Karam, Lebanese singer
- February 27 – Alison Gertz, American AIDS activist (d. 1992)

- February 28 – Ickey Woods, former NFL running back famous for the Ickey Shuffle

March

Zack Snyder

- March 1 – Zack Snyder, American actor, film director, screenwriter, and producer
- March 2
    - Sheren Tang, Hong Kong actress
    - David Wickham, British concert pianist, musical director and conductor
- March 3
    - Tone Lōc, African-American R&B musician
    - Nick Rhodes, British scientist
- March 4
    - Daniela Amavia, American actress and international model
    - Ant Banks, African-American rapper
    - Steve Bastoni, Australian actor
    - Kevin Johnson, American basketball player
    - Dav Pilkey, American writer
    - Wash Westmoreland, British film director
- March 5

- o Mark Z. Danielewski, American author
- o Michael Irvin, American football player
- March 6 – Maurice Ashley, American chess grandmaster
- March 7
  - o Jeff Feagles, American football kicker
  - o Atsushi Sakurai, Japanese singer (Buck-Tick)
- March 8 – Fabian Cairns, Chairperson of the Graaf Reinet chamber of commerce, founder of Nautilus Shipbroking and FJ livestock feeds
- March 9 – Tony Lockett, Australian rules footballer
- March 10
  - o Edie Brickell, American singer
  - o Mike Timlin, American baseball player
- March 16 – Rodney Peete, African-American football quarterback
- March 17 – Espen Hammer, Norwegian Philosopher
- March 18 – Anne Will, German television journalist
- March 19 – Nigel Clough, English footballer
- March 21 – Roy G. Niederhoffer, Investment Manager
- March 22 – Antonio Pinto, Portuguese long-distance runner
- March 25
  - o Tom Glavine, American baseball player
  - o Jeff Healey, Canadian guitarist (d. 2008)
  - o Anton Rogan, Northern Irish footballer
- March 26 – Michael Imperioli, American actor
- March 28 – Cheryl James, African-American rapper (Salt-n-Pepa)
- March 29 – Krasimir Balakov, Bulgarian footballer

April

Chris Evans

Robin Wright

Samantha Fox

- April 1 – Chris Evans, British radio disc-jockey
- April 2 – Teddy Sheringham, British footballer
- April 3
    - Michael Mittermeier, German comedian
    - Miina Tominaga, Japanese voice actress

- April 4
  - Riduan Isamuddin, Bali bombing suspect
  - Mike Starr, American bassist (Alice in Chains) (d. 2011)
- April 8
  - Bobby Ologun, Nigerian television personality and martial artist
  - Robin Wright, American actress
- April 9 – John Hammond, British weather forecaster
- April 11 – Lisa Stansfield, British soul singer
- April 13 – Ali Boumnijel, Tunisian footballer
- April 14
  - David Justice, African-American baseball player
  - Greg Maddux, American baseball player
- April 15 – Samantha Fox, British model and singer
- April 18 – Trine Hattestad, Norwegian athlete
- April 19
  - El Samurai, Japanese professional wrestler
  - Oliver Welke, German television presenter, actor, comedian and sports journalist
- April 20 – David Chalmers, Australian philosopher
- April 22
  - Dana Barron, American actress
  - Jeffrey Dean Morgan, American actor
- April 25
  - Man Arenas, Spanish comic creator
  - Tim Easton, American songwriter
- April 26 – Natasha Trethewey, Pulitzer Prize–winning poet
- April 27
  - Siw Anita Andersen Norwegian actress
  - Yoshihiro Togashi, Japanese author and illustrator

- April 28
    - John Daly, American golfer
    - Ali-Reza Pahlavi, titular prince of Iran (d. 2011)
- April 29 – Phil Tufnell, British cricketer

May

Helena Bonham Carter

Janet Jackson

Stephen Baldwin

Darius Rucker

- May 3 – Firdous Bamji, Indian-American actor
- May 5 – Lyubov Yegorova, Russian cross-country skier
- May 6
  - Andrea Chiesa, Swiss Formula One driver
  - Cindy Hsu, American Emmy-Award-winning journalist
- May 7
  - Anderson Cummins, Canadian cricketer
  - Jes Høgh, Danish footballer
- May 8
  - Robert J. Behnen, American genealogist and a former member of the Missouri House of Representatives
  - Kamil Kašťák, Czech ice hockey player
  - Marta Sánchez, Spanish female vocalist, entertainer
  - Rocko Schamoni, German entertainer, author, musician, club proprietor and member of the comedy ensemble Studio Braun
  - Cláudio Taffarel, Brazilian goalkeeper
- May 10
  - Mikael Andersson, Swedish ice hockey player
  - Jonathan Edwards, British athlete

- o Anne Elvebakk, Norwegian biathlete
- o Genaro Hernández, Mexican-American boxer
- May 12
  - o Stephen Baldwin, American actor
  - o Dez Fafara, American singer
  - o Bebel Gilberto, Brazilian popular singer
- May 13
  - o Nereus Acosta, Filipino politician, academician, and political scientist
  - o Cheryl Dunye, Liberian-born film director, producer, screenwriter, editor and actress
  - o Alison Goldfrapp, English musician, Goldfrapp.
  - o Darius Rucker, African-American country singer
- May 14 – Raphael Saadiq, American singer-songwriter
- May 16
  - o Juan Manuel Funes, Guatemalan footballer and coach
  - o Janet Jackson, African-American singer
  - o Thurman Thomas, American football player
- May 17 – Hill Harper, American actor
- May 19 – Sophia Crawford, actress, stuntwoman and martial artist
- May 20
  - o Mindy Cohn, American actress and comedienne
  - o Joey Gamache, American boxer
- May 21
  - o Lisa Edelstein, American actress and playwright
  - o François Omam-Biyik, Cameroonian football player
- May 22
  - o Siri Eftedal, Norwegian team handball player and Olympic medalist

- Johnny Gill, American singer
- May 23
  - H Jon Benjamin, American actor and comedian
  - Graeme Hick, English cricketer
- May 24
  - Eric Cantona, French footballer
  - Francisco Javier Cruz, Mexican football player
  - Ricky Craven, American race car driver and sportscaster
  - Russell Kun, Nauruan politician
- May 25
  - Ahmad Reza Abedzadeh, Iranian goalkeeper
  - Jeff Cross, American football player
- May 26
  - Helena Bonham Carter, English actress
  - Zola Budd, South African athlete
- May 27
  - Heston Blumenthal, British chef
  - Carol Campbell, Afro-German actress, model and presenter
  - Sean Kinney, drummer for the rock band Alice in Chains
  - Titi DJ, Indonesian pop singer
- May 28
  - Theo Bleckmann, German vocalist and composer
  - Larry Davis, American criminal (d. 2008)
- May 29 – Robert Anderson, American child murderer (executed) (d. 2006)
- May 30
  - Frank Goosen, German cabaret artist and novel author

○ Thomas Häßler, German football player

June

Emmanuelle Seigner

John Cusack

Mike Tyson

- June 2 – Candace Gingrich, American LGBT rights activist
- June 3 – Wasim Akram, Pakistani cricketer

- June 4 – Cecilia Bartoli, Italian mezzo-soprano
- June 6 – Faure Gnassingbé, President of Togo
- June 8
  - Jens Kidman, Swedish musician
  - Julianna Margulies, American actress
- June 13 – Grigori Perelman, Russian mathematician
- June 14
  - Matt Freeman, American musician
  - Indira Radić, Bosnian Serb singer
  - Eduardo Waghorn, Chilean musician
- June 15 – Roberto Carnevale, Italian musician
- June 16
  - Phil Vischer, American voice actor, puppeteer, writer, animator, creator of VeggieTales.
  - Jan Železný, Czech javelin thrower
- June 18 – Kurt Browning, Canadian figure skater
- June 19 – Samuel West, British actor
- June 21 – Rudi Bakhtiar, American journalist
- June 22
  - Michael Park, British rally co-driver (d. 2005)
  - Emmanuelle Seigner, French actress
- June 23
  - Richie Jen, Taiwanese musician
  - Eric Thomas, Inventor of LISTSERV
- June 25 – Dikembe Mutombo, Congolese basketball player
- June 27 – J. J. Abrams, American television writer and producer
- June 28
  - John Cusack, American actor
  - Mary Stuart Masterson, American actress

- June 30
  - Cheryl Bernard, Canadian Olympic curler
  - Marton Csokas, New Zealand actor
  - Mike Tyson, African-American boxer

July

Tamsin Greig

Enrique Peña Nieto

Tim Brown

- July 1 – Enrico Annoni, Italian footballer
- July 3
  - Moisés Alou, American baseball player
  - Robin Burgener, Canadian programmer, inventor of 20Q
- July 5
  - Claudia Wells, American actress
  - Gianfranco Zola, Italian footballer
- July 6 – Brian Posehn, American actor and comedian
- July 7 – Gundula Krause, German violinist
- July 8
  - Ralf Altmeyer, German virologist
  - Shadlog Bernicke, Nauruan politician
- July 10 – Gina Bellman, British actress
- July 11
  - Mick Molloy, Australian comedian
  - Kentaro Miura, Japanese author and illustrator
- July 12 – Tamsin Greig, English actress
- July 14 – Matthew Fox, American actor
- July 15
  - Irène Jacob, French-born actress
  - Samuel Rosa, Brazilian singer-songwriter of the band Skank
- July 20 – Enrique Peña Nieto, President of Mexico, Governor of the State of Mexico (2005–2011)
- July 21 – Sarah Waters, British novelist
- July 22 – Tim Brown, American football player
- July 25 – Wataru Takagi, Japanese voice actor
- July 28
  - Miguel Ángel Nadal, Spanish footballer

- Shikao Suga, Japanese singer
- July 29 – Richard Steven Horvitz, American voice actor
- July 30
  - Murilo Bustamante, Brazilian mixed martial artist
  - Allan Langer, Australian rugby league footballer
- July 31 – Dean Cain, American actor

August

Jimmy Wales

Halle Berry

Rodney Mullen

- August 2 – Tim Wakefield, American baseball player
- August 3 – Brent Butt, Canadian comedian and TV producer
- August 4 – Kensuke Sasaki, Japanese professional wrestler
- August 7 – Jimmy Wales, American co-founder of Wikipedia
- August 10
    - Charlie Dimmock, English TV gardening expert
    - Hossam Hassan, Egyptian footballer
- August 11 – Juan María Solare, Argentine composer
- August 12 – Les Ferdinand, English footballer
- August 14
    - Halle Berry, African-American actress
    - Freddy Rincón, Colombian footballer
- August 15 – Scott Brosius, American baseball player
- August 17 – Rodney Mullen, American skateboarder
- August 19 – Lee Ann Womack, American musician
- August 20 – Enrico Letta, Italian Prime Minister
- August 23 – Rik Smits, Dutch basketball player
- August 25
    - Robert Maschio, American actor
    - Sandra Maischberger, German journalist, talk show host, and author
- August 26 – Jacques Brinkman, Dutch field hockey player
- August 27
    - Jeroen Duyster, Dutch rower
    - Juhan Parts, Estonian Prime Minister
- August 28 – Priya Dutt, Indian social worker and politician

September

Salma Hayek

Toby Jones

Carola Häggkvist

Adam Sandler

- September 1 – Tim Hardaway, American basketball player
- September 2 – Salma Hayek, Mexican-American actress
- September 4 – Yanka Dyagileva, Russian singer
- September 6 – Eduardo Maruri, Ecuadorian businessman and politician
- September 7
  - Vladimir Andreyev, Russian race walker
  - Toby Jones, English actor
  - Gunda Niemann-Stirnemann, German speed skater
- September 8 – Carola Häggkvist, Swedish pop singer, Eurovision Song Contest 1991 winner
- September 9
  - Georg Hackl, German luger
  - Adam Sandler, American actor and comedian
- September 12 – Princess Akishino of Japan
- September 19 – Soledad O'Brien, American television journalist and news anchor
- September 20 – Nuno Bettencourt, Portuguese-American guitarist and singer-songwriter
- September 21 – James Richardson, English television presenter and journalist

- September 22
  - Moustafa Amar, Egyptian singer
  - Mike Richter, American ice hockey player
- September 24 – Michael J. Varhola, American author and publisher
- September 25 – Jason Flemyng, English actor

October

David Cameron

Luke Perry

Jon Favreau

Roman Abramovich

Zoran Milanović

- October 1 – George Weah, Liberian politician and football player
- October 2 – Rodney Anoa'i, Samoan-American professional wrestler (d. 2000)

- October 3 – Rabbi Binyamin Ze'ev Kahane, Israeli settler leader (d. 2000)
- October 5 – Inessa Kravets, Ukrainian athlete
- October 6 – Niall Quinn, Irish footballer
- October 7 – Sherman Alexie, Native American author
- October 8 – Aaron Callaghan, Irish football club executive
- October 9 – David Cameron, British Prime Minister
- October 10
  - Tony Adams, English footballer
  - Bai Ling, Chinese actress
  - Elana Meyer, South African athlete
- October 11
  - Luke Perry, American actor
  - Stephen Williams, British politician
- October 12 – Brian Kennedy, Northern Irish musician and author
- October 14 – Savanna Samson, American porn star
- October 15
  - Eric Benet, African-American singer and songwriter
  - Jorge Campos, Mexican footballer and coach
- October 16 – Mary Elizabeth McGlynn, American voice actress
- October 18 – Angela Visser, Miss Universe 1989
- October 19 – Jon Favreau, American actor and director
- October 20 – Stefan Raab, German entertainer, television host, comedian, and musician
- October 22 – Valeria Golino, Italian-Greek film and television actress
- October 24 – Roman Abramovich, UK-based Russian billionaire businessman

- October 25 – Wendel Clark, Canadian hockey player
- October 27 – Matt Drudge, American conservative journalist
- October 28
  - Steve Atwater, American football player
  - Andy Richter, American actor, writer, comedian, and late night talk show announcer
- October 30 – Zoran Milanović, Prime Minister of Croatia
- October 31
  - Adam Horovitz, American rapper (Beastie Boys)
  - Koji Kanemoto, Japanese professional wrestler
  - Mike O'Malley, American actor and playwright

November

David Schwimmer

Gordon Ramsay

Vincent Cassel

- November 2
  - Yoshinari Ogawa, Japanese professional wrestler
  - David Schwimmer, American actor
- November 3 – Joe Hachem, Lebanese-born Australian poker player
- November 6
  - Kae Araki, Japanese voice actress
  - Christian Lorenz, German rock musician (*Rammstein*)
- November 8 – Gordon Ramsay, Scottish chef, restaurateur, and television personality
- November 10 – Vanessa Angel, English model and actress
- November 13 – Susanna Haapoja, Finnish politician (d. 2009)
- November 14 – Curt Schilling, American baseball player
- November 15 – Rachel True, American actress
- November 17
  - Jeff Buckley, American singer-songwriter (d. 1997)
  - Daisy Fuentes, Cuban-born American model and television personality
  - Sophie Marceau, French actress
- November 19 – Shmuley Boteach, American rabbi

- November 21 – Troy Aikman, American sports commentator and former pro football player
- November 23 – Vincent Cassel, French actor
- November 25
  - Tim Armstrong, American singer-songwriter
  - Billy Burke, American actor
- November 28 – Narumi Yasuda, Japanese actress
- November 29 – John Bradshaw Layfield, American professional wrestler
- November 30
  - Wil Mara, American author
  - David Nicholls, English novelist and screenwriter

December

Patricia Kaas

Sinéad O'Connor

Helle Thorning-Schmidt

Kiefer Sutherland

- December 1 – Larry Walker, Canadian Major League Baseball player
- December 4 – Fred Armisen, American actor, comedian and musician
- December 5 – Patricia Kaas, French singer and actress
- December 7
    - C. Thomas Howell, American actor
    - Linn Ullmann, Norwegian journalist and author
- December 8 – Sinéad O'Connor, Irish pop singer
- December 9
    - Tim Bull, Australian politician
    - Michael Foster, drummer for rock band FireHouse
    - Montserrat Gil Torné, Andorran politician
    - Kirsten Gillibrand, American politician
    - Dave Harold, English professional snooker player
    - Toby Huss, American actor
    - Dana Murzyn, Canadian hockey player
    - Spencer Rochfort, Canadian-American actor
    - Julio Alberto Rodas Hurtarte, former soccer player

- o Mateo Romero, Native American painter
- o Gideon Sa'ar, Israeli politician
- o Kadyrbek Sarbayev, foreign minister of Kyrgyzstan
- o Shane Scott, American director, writer, producer, cinematographer, editor, musician
- o Martin Taylor, footballer coach
- o Natee Thongsookkaew, Thailand footballer
- December 11
  - o Gary Dourdan, American actor
  - o Leon Lai, Hong Kong singer and actor
- December 12
  - o Royce Gracie, Brazilian martial artist
  - o Greg Long, American Christian musician
  - o Último Dragón, Japanese professional wrestler
  - o Lydia Zimmermann, Spanish filmmaker
- December 13 – Don Roff, American writer and filmmaker
- December 14
  - o Bill Ranford, Canadian hockey player
  - o Helle Thorning-Schmidt, Danish Prime Minister
  - o Anthony Mason, American basketball player (d. 2015)
- December 15 – Katja von Garnier, German film director
- December 16 – Dennis Wise, English footballer
- December 17 – Miloš Tichý, Czech astronomer
- December 19
  - o Tim Sköld, Swedish multi-instrumentalist musician
  - o Alberto Tomba, Italian alpine skier
- December 20 – Ed de Goeij, Dutch footballer
- December 21 – Kiefer Sutherland, Canadian actor
- December 22 – Dmitry Bilozerchev, Soviet gymnast
- December 25 – Stephen Twigg, British politician

- December 26 – Jay Yuenger, American musician and producer
- December 27 – Bill Goldberg, American professional wrestler
- December 28 – Kaliopi, Macedonian singer-songwriter
- December 30 – Eric Kot, Hong Kong singer and actor

Date unknown

- Sharon D. Clarke, British theatre and television actress and singer
- Kivi Larmola, Finnish artist

Deaths

January

Vincent Auriol

Hannes Kolehmainen

- January 1
  - Vincent Auriol, President of France (b. 1884)

- o W. W. Burnside, American plantation owner and politician (b. 1882)
- o Oscar Dugey, American baseball player (b. 1887)
- o George Featherstone, Australian rules footballer (b. 1889)
- January 2
  - o Haps Benfer, American football and basketball player and coach (b. 1893)
  - o Jan Gadomski, Polish astronomer (b. 1889)
- January 3
  - o Haidar Abashidze, Georgian politician, journalist, and educator (b. 1893)
  - o Luther Bonin, American baseball player (b. 1888)
  - o Henry James Forman, American writer (b. 1879)
  - o Marguerite Higgins, American journalist (b. 1920)
  - o Rex Lease, American actor (b. 1903)
- January 4
  - o Inga Artamonova, Soviet speed skater (b. 1936)
  - o Marshall Caffyn, Australian rules footballer (b. 1892)
  - o Arthur Charlesworth, English footballer (b. 1898)
  - o Cecil Copping, American composer (b. 1888)
  - o John F. Dittbrender, American politician, Member of the Wisconsin State Assembly (b. 1878)
  - o Guido Fiorini, Italian art director (b. 1897)
  - o Seiko Fujita, Japanese martial artist (b. 1898)
- January 5
  - o Mirashi Buwa, Indian classical singer (b. 1883)
  - o Richard C. Dillon, American politician, Governor of New Mexico (b. 1877)
  - o George Duckworth, English cricketer (b. 1901)

- January 6
  - Albrecht Brandi, German U-boat commander in World War II (b. 1914)
  - Harmar D. Denny, Jr., American politician, member of the U.S. House of Representatives from Pennsylvania (b. 1886)
  - James Lawrence Fly, American lawyer, Chairman of the Federal Communications Commission (b. 1898)
- January 7
  - Ernest Bernau, New Zealand cricketer (b. 1896)
  - Allan Chapman, Scottish politician, MP (b. 1897)
- January 8 – Marthe Cnockaert, Belgian spy during World War I (b. 1892)
- January 9
  - Eusebio Rodolfo Cordón Cea, provisional president of El Salvador (b. 1899)
  - Friedrich Wilhelm Foerster, German-French-American philosopher (b. 1869)
- January 10
  - Fen Cresswell, New Zealand cricketer (b. 1915)
  - Vernon Dahmer, American civil rights leader (b. 1908)
  - Nishizō Tsukahara, Japanese admiral (b. 1887)
- January 11
  - Joseph William Comeau, Canadian politician, member of the Senate of Canada (b. 1876)
  - Robin de la Condamine, English actor (b. 1877)
  - Alberto Giacometti, Swiss sculptor (b. 1901)
  - Hannes Kolehmainen, Finnish runner (b. 1889)
  - Lal Bahadur Shastri, Prime Minister of India (b. 1904)
- January 12

- o Norman Emerson, Irish Anglican priest and author (b. 1900)
- o Narhar Vishnu Gadgil, Indian politician, Minister of Public Works (b. 1896)
- January 13
  - o Johan Arnd Aasgaard, American Lutheran church leader (b. 1876)
  - o Leopoldo Baracco, Italian politician, member of Constituent Assembly of Italy and of the Chamber of Deputies (b. 1886)
  - o Flora Jean Cameron, New Zealand nurse (b. 1902)
- January 14
  - o Curt Backeberg, German horticulturist (b. 1894)
  - o Beatrice Mary Barth, New Zealand piano teacher (b. 1877)
  - o Bill Carr, American athlete, Olympic gold medalist in 1932 (b. 1909)
  - o Lella Secor Florence, American writer and activist (b. 1887)
- January 15
  - o Samuel Akintola, Nigerian premier of the Western region and Aare Ona Kakanfo XIII of the Yoruba (b. 1910)
  - o Charles Elliot Allen, Irish rugby union forward (b. 1880)
  - o Sir Ahmadu Bello, Nigerian politician, first premier of the Northern Nigeria region (b. 1910)
  - o Birger Braadland, Norwegian politician, Minister of Foreign Affairs (b. 1879)
  - o Stiles O. Clements, American architect (b. 1883)

- Sergei Korolev, Russian space scientist (b. 1907)
- January 16
  - Raynold E. Acre, American aviation pioneer (b. 1889)
  - Nikolai Bernstein, Soviet neurophysiologist (b. 1896)
  - Johnny Broderick, American police detective in New York City (b. 1896)
  - Bobby Burns, American actor and director (b. 1878)
  - Archibald Bush, American businessman (b. 1887)
- January 17
  - Percival Barnett, English cricketer (b. 1889)
  - Edward Craigie, Australian politician, member of the South Australian House of Assembly (b. 1871)
  - Vincent J. Donehue, American stage director (b. 1917)
  - Georges Figon, French secret agent
  - Otto Flügel, German submariner (b. 1917)
- January 18
  - Hyacinthe-Adélard Fortier, Canadian politician, member of the Canadian House of Commons (b. 1875)
  - Kathleen Norris, American writer (b. 1880)
- January 19
  - Henry Ah Kew, New Zealand lawyer and community leader (b. 1900)
  - Violet Bathurst, Lady Apsley, British Conservative Party politician, MP (b. 1895)
  - James Carmichael, British politician, MP (b. 1894)
  - Édouard Paul Dhorme, French Semitologist (b. 1881)
  - Frank Foyston, Canadian ice hockey player (b. 1891)
- January 20
  - Bill Anderton, New Zealand Labour Party politician (b. 1891)

- o George Devine, English theatrical producer, manager, actor (b. 1910)
- January 21
  - o Pol Abraham, French architect (b. 1891)
  - o Robert Beasley, British cricketer (b. 1882)
  - o Sir Richard Layton Butler, Australian politician, Premier of South Australia (b. 1885)
  - o Paul Comtois, Canadian politician, Lieutenant Governor of Quebec (b. 1895)
  - o William Davies, Welsh footballer (b. 1882)
  - o Mary Teresa Enright, New Zealand educator (b. 1880)
- January 22
  - o Cyril Dugmore, British athlete, competed at the 1908 Summer Olympics (b. 1882)
  - o Jean Galtier-Boissière, French writer (b. 1891)
  - o Herbert Marshall, English actor (b. 1890)
- January 23
  - o Jo van Ammers-Küller, Dutch writer (b. 1884)
  - o Frank L. Anders, United States Army soldier, received Medal of Honor (b. 1875)
  - o Berton Braley, American poet (b. 1882)
  - o Pat Cannon, American politician, United States Representative from Florida (b. 1904)
  - o Martin Conlon, Irish politician, TD (b. 1879)
- January 24
  - o Homi J. Bhabha, Indian nuclear physicist, known as "father of the Indian nuclear programme" (b. 1909)
  - o David Brynmor Anthony, Welsh academic administrator (b. 1886)
- January 25

- Saul Adler FRS, Russian-born British-Israeli expert on parasitology (b. 1895)
- Edmund Blaurock, German Army general during World War II (b. 1899)
- Miguel Bover, Spanish bicycle racer (b. 1928)
- Alfred Cliff, English cricketer (b. 1878)
- Bradshaw Crandell, American artist (b. 1896)
- January 26
  - Robert Corkey, Northern Ireland politician and Presbyterian minister (b. 1881)
  - Stanton Crawford, American academic, Chancellor of the University of Pittsburgh (b. 1897)
- January 27
  - Caterina Albert, Spanish writer (b. 1869)
  - Major Ronald Armstrong-Jones, British barrister and soldier; father-in-law of Princess Margaret (b. 1899)
  - Grover Cleveland Bergdoll, American pilot who went to Germany to avoid service in World War I (b. 1893)
  - Norman Blackburn, English World War I pilot and aviation industrialist (b. 1896)
  - Henry Carlton Cumberbatch, British Royal Navy officer during World War II (b. 1900)
- January 28
  - Benjamin Burrows, English composer (b. 1891)
  - Victims of Lufthansa Flight 005:
    - Bruno Bianchi, Italian swimmer, competitor at 1960 and 1964 Olympic Games (b. 1943)
    - Paolo Costoli, Italian swimmer, competed at 1928 Olympics and 1932 Olympics (b. 1910)

- Dino Rora, Italian swimmer, competed at 1964 Olympics (b. 1945)
- January 29
  - Sir George Barstow KCB, British civil servant and businessman (b. 1874)
  - Robert Elias Fries, Swedish botanist (b. 1876)
- January 30
  - Erik Bergström, Swedish footballer, Olympic competitor in 1908 and 1912 (b. 1886)
  - Florence St John Cadell, Scottish artist (b. 1877)
  - Harry Curtis, English footballer and manager (b. 1890)
  - Charlie Foletta, Australian rules footballer (b. 1875)
- January 31
  - Karl Björkänge, Swedish politician, member of parliament (b. 1895)
  - Dirk Brouwer, Dutch-American astronomer (b. 1902)
  - Manishi Dey, Indian painter (b. 1909)
  - Pat Donahue, American baseball player (b. 1884)
  - Elizabeth Patterson, American actress (b. 1875)

February

Buster Keaton

- February 1
  - Roswell M. Austin, American politician and attorney; Speaker of the Vermont House of Representatives (b. 1887)
  - Charles Belden, American photographer (b. 1887)
  - Stuart Campbell, British journalist and editor (b. 1908)
  - Arthur Curle, British cricketer (b. 1895)
  - Gen. John D'Arcy, British Army officer (b. 1894)
  - Hedda Hopper, American gossip columnist (b. 1885)
  - Buster Keaton, American actor and film director (b. 1895)
  - Joseph R. Knowland, American politician and newspaper publisher (b. 1873)
- February 3
  - Gianni Di Venanzo, Italian cinematographer (b. 1920)
  - Kamil Abdul Rahim, Egyptian diplomat (b. 1897)
  - June Walker, American actress (b. 1900)
- February 4
  - Lucius Beebe, American author and syndicated columnist (b. 1902)
  - Ady Berber, Austrian film actor (b. 1913)
  - Sir Lance Brisbane, Australian businessman (b. 1893)
  - Irvin Brooks, American baseball player (b. 1891)
  - Charles Comber, Australian rules footballer (b. 1891)
  - Howard Dea, Canadian ice hockey player (b. 1891)
- February 5
  - Ludwig Binswanger, Swiss psychiatrist, pioneer in existential psychology (b. 1881)
  - John Breen, Australian politician, Member of the Australian House of Representatives (b. 1898)

- February 6
  - Paul Bardal, Canadian politician, member of the Legislative Assembly of Manitoba (b. 1889)
  - Wayne G. Borah, United States federal judge (b. 1891)
  - Narcisa de Leon, Filipino film mogul (b. 1877)
- February 7 – Bill Dole, American football coach (b. 1909)
- February 8
  - Vernon Andrade, American jazz bandleader active primarily in New York City in the 1920s and 1930s (b. 1902)
  - William L. Clayton, American Under Secretary of State (b. 1880)
  - James Creese, American academic administrator (b. 1896)
  - Paul Sophus Epstein, Polish-born Russian-American mathematical physicist (b. 1883)
- February 9
  - Bruno Ahlberg, Finnish boxer, Olympic athlete (*1932* and *1936*) (b. 1911)
  - Giovanni Benfratello, Italian fencer, competitor at the 1912 Summer Olympics (b. 1888)
  - Budd Fine, American actor (b. 1894)
  - Sophie Tucker, American singer (b. 1884)
- February 10
  - Theodor Beckmann, German Luftwaffe officer during World War II (b. 1897)
  - Bruno Bitkowski, Canadian all-star football centre (*Ottawa Rough Riders*) (b. 1929)
  - Ryan DeGraffenried, Sr., American politician, member of the Alabama House of Representatives (b. 1925)

- William Dillon, American songwriter (b. 1877)
- Adm. Sir John Edelsten, British Royal Navy admiral (b. 1891)
- Gen. J. F. C. Fuller, British Army general during World War I (b. 1878)
- Billy Rose, American composer and band leader (b. 1899)
- February 11
  - Reginald Boden, English cricketer (b. 1884)
  - Fred E. Busbey, American politician, U.S. Representative from Illinois (b. 1895)
  - Victor-Stanislas Chartrand, Canadian politician, member of the Legislative Assembly of Quebec (b. 1887)
- February 12 – Leon Beer, Australian rules footballer (b. 1903)
- February 13 – Roy Crisp, Australian rules footballer (b. 1890)
- February 14
  - Hugo Björne, Swedish actor (b. 1886)
  - Germain Caron, Canadian politician, Member of the Legislative Assembly of Quebec (b. 1910)
  - Charles Chellapah, Singaporean photojournalist (b. 1939)
  - Jack Coffey, American baseball player (b. 1887)
  - Adrian Cole, Australian Air Vice Marshal (b. 1895)
  - François Demol, Belgian footballer (b. 1895)
  - Ernest Albert Egerton, English soldier, recipient of the Victoria Cross (b. 1897)
  - Charles Elsey, British race horse trainer (b. 1882)
- February 15

- o James B. Allardice, American television comedy writer of the 1950s and 1960s (b. 1919)
- o Sir Abubakar Tafawa Balewa, Prime Minister of Nigeria (b. 1912)
- o Venceslau Brás, President of Brazil (b. 1868)
- o Spence Burton, American-born Anglican bishop of Nassau, Bahamas (b. 1881)
- o Gerard Ciołek, Polish architect and historian of gardens (b. 1909)
- o Hedwig Conrad-Martius, German phenomenologist and mystic (b. 1888)
- o Armando Fizzarotti, Italian screenwriter and film director (b. 1892)
- February 16
  - o Georgi Belev, Bulgarian opera singer (b. 1908)
  - o Paul Henri Bouffard, Canadian politician, member of the Senate of Canada (b. 1895)
  - o John Thomas Davies, English Anglican priest (b. 1881)
  - o Károly Escher, Hungarian photographer (b. 1890)
- February 17
  - o Siegmund Beutum, Austrian chess master (b. 1890)
  - o Syd Carman, Australian rules footballer (b. 1901)
  - o Chen Shutong, Chinese politician (b. 1876)
  - o Mike Chornohus, Austria-Hungary-born Canadian politician, member of the Legislative Assembly of Alberta (b. 1888)
  - o Hans Hofmann, German-American painter (b. 1880)
- February 18

- Mary Patricia Anderson, New Zealand politician, one of the first two women appointed to the New Zealand Legislative Council (b. 1887)
- Heinz Baader, German Luftwaffe officer during World War II (b. 1916)
- James Harry Beatty, Canadian politician, member of the Legislative Assembly of British Columbia (b. 1890)
- Rick Bockelie, Norwegian sailor, gold medalist at the 1924 Summer Olympics (b. 1902)
- Carol Ann Drazba, American military nurse killed in Vietnam War (b. 1943)
- Daniel D. Fernández, American soldier, recipient of the Medal of Honor (b. 1944)
- Robert Rossen, American film director (b. 1908)
- February 20
  - Solomon Asch, Polish gestalt psychologist and pioneer in social psychology in the United States (b. 1907)
  - Fernand Francell, French opera singer and actor (b. 1880)
  - Chester W. Nimitz, American admiral (b. 1885)
- February 22
  - Everitt P. Blizard, Canadian-born American nuclear physicist and engineer (b. 1916)
  - Bernard Braskamp, American Presbyterian minister, Chaplain of the United States House of Representatives (b. 1887)
  - Georg Erdmann, Norwegian sports shooter, competed in the 1908 Summer Olympics (b. 1875)
- February 24 – Jean d'Esme, French writer (b. 1894)
- February 25

- ○ Garland Braxton, American baseball player (b. 1900)
- ○ Ira Delbert Cotnam, Canadian politician, member of the Canadian House of Commons (b. 1883)
- ○ Melchor Fernández Almagro, Spanish writer (b. 1893)
- ○ G. C. Foster, Jamaican sportsman (b. 1885)
- February 26
  - ○ José María Albareda, Spanish scientist, Secretary General and head of the Higher Council of Scientific Research (CSIC) (b. 1902)
  - ○ Emiliano Chamorro Vargas, President of Nicaragua (b. 1871)
  - ○ Sir Guy Dain, English physician (b. 1870)
  - ○ Adm. Richard Bell Davies, British Royal Navy officer and recipient of the Victoria Cross (b. 1886)
  - ○ Les Davis, American football coach (b. 1900)
  - ○ Gino Severini, Italian painter (b. 1883)
- February 27 – Curt Badinski, German Wehrmacht general during World War II (b. 1890)
- February 28
  - ○ Charles Bassett, American test pilot and NASA astronaut (b. 1931)
  - ○ Schamyl Bauman, Swedish film director (b. 1893)
  - ○ George Harrison Dunbar, Canadian politician, member of the Legislative Assembly of Ontario (b. 1878)
  - ○ Jonathan Hale, American actor (b. 1891)

March

- March 1
  - ○ Hugh Baillie, American journalist, head of UP (b. 1890)

- George William Chafer, English recipient of the Victoria Cross (b. 1894)
- Károly Csapkay, Hungarian footballer and manager (b. 1894)
- Arthur Henry Davey, New Zealand master mariner (b. 1878)
- Rick Decker, American race car driver (b. 1903)
- Karel Dostal, Czech actor (b. 1884)
- Adm. Sir John Eccles, English Royal Navy admiral (b. 1898)
- Fritz Houtermans, German physicist (b. 1903)
- William R. Munroe, American admiral (b. 1886)
- Donald Stewart, American-born English actor (b. 1910)
- March 2 – Vincent Fanelli, American musician (b. 1881)
- March 3
  - Alfonso Castaldo, Italian Cardinal of the Roman Catholic Church, Archbishop of Naples (b. 1890)
  - Peter S. Connor, American marine, received the Medal of Honor (b. 1932)
  - Bernard Charles Cotton, English-born Australian malacologist (b. 1905)
  - Joseph Fields, American playwright (b. 1895)
  - Jack Fier, American film producer (b. 1896)
  - William Frawley, American actor (*I Love Lucy*) (b. 1887)
  - Maxfield Parrish, American artist (b. 1870)
  - Alice Pearce, American actress (b. 1917)
- March 4
  - Stanley Anderson, English artist (b. 1884)
  - Joseph Fields, American playwright, theatre director, screenwriter, and film producer (b. 1895)

- March 5 – Anna Akhmatova, Russian poet (b. 1889)
- March 6
    - Louis-Mathias Auger, Canadian teacher and Liberal Party politician, member of the Canadian House of Commons (b. 1902)
    - Charles F. Buddy, American Roman Catholic Bishop of San Diego (b. 1887)
    - Giorgio Bulgari, Italian businessman (*Bulgari*) (b. 1890)
    - Michitaro Totsuka, Japanese admiral (b. 1890)
- March 7
    - William Astor, 3rd Viscount Astor, English businessman and Conservative Party politician (b. 1907)
    - Donald B. Beary, American admiral (b. 1888)
    - Bill Cahill, Australian rules footballer (b. 1911)
    - George Camsell, English footballer (b. 1902)
    - Sir Nigel Colman, 1st Baronet, British politician, MP (b. 1886)
    - Hilding Ekman, Swedish runner, competed at the 1920 Summer Olympics (b. 1893)
    - Georg Faber, German mathematician (b. 1877)
- March 8
    - Sir John Blake-Reed, British judge (b. 1882)
    - Roger L. Dell, American jurist, Chief Justice of Minnesota (b. 1897)
    - Roderick Falconer, English cricketer (b. 1886)
- March 9
    - John F. Baldwin, Jr., American politician, U.S. Representative from California (b. 1915)

- René Barbier, French fencer, silver medalist at the 1928 Summer Olympics (b. 1891)
- Pablo Birger, Argentine racing driver (b. 1924)
- George Cornell, English criminal (b. *c.* 1928)
- March 10
  - Walter Heywood Bryan, Australian geologist (b. 1891)
  - Émile Coulonvaux, Belgian lawyer and politician (b. 1892)
  - Frank O'Connor, Irish writer (b. 1903)
  - Frits Zernike, Dutch physicist, Nobel Prize laureate (b. 1888)
- March 11
  - James Barnhill, American football official (b. 1921)
  - James E. Fitzsimmons, American racehorse trainer (b. 1874)
- March 12
  - Victor Brauner, Romanian artist (b. 1903)
  - George Caldwell, American builder (b. 1892)
  - Sir Sydney Camm, English aeronautical engineer (b. 1893)
- March 13
  - Guido Bruck, Austrian numismatist (b. 1920)
  - Max Clara, Italian-born German anatomist (b. 1899)
  - Johnny Duncan, Scottish footballer (b. 1896)
- March 15
  - Osendé Afana, Cameroonian guerrilla (b. 1930)
  - Ruth Dalton, British politician, MP (b. 1890)
  - Yenovk Der Hagopian, Turkish-born American artist (b. 1900)

- James Donahue, American pentathlete, silver medalist at 1912 Summer Olympics (b. 1885)
- Norman Augustus Finch, English sergeant in the Royal Marines, recipient of the Victoria Cross (b. 1890)
- March 16 – Joseph-Odilon Duval, Canadian politician, member of the Legislative Assembly of Quebec (b. 1895)
- March 17 – Don Eagle, Canadian wrestler (b. 1925)
- March 18
  - Frank Bennett, American baseball player (Boston Red Sox) (b. 1904)
  - John Gaha, Australian politician, member of the Australian House of Representatives (b. 1894)
- March 19 – Erik Aaes, Danish set designer and art director (b. 1899)
- March 20
  - Laurence Abrams, English professional footballer (b. 1889)
  - Demetrios Galanis, Greek artist (b. 1879)
  - Johnny Morrison, professional baseball player (b. 1895)
- March 21
  - Norman Coates, British army officer and politician, MP (b. 1890)
  - Tom Fern, English footballer (b. 1886)
  - Frank Finnan, Australian politician, member of the New South Wales Legislative Assembly (B. 1897)
- March 22
  - Bruno Bieler, German general during World War II (b. 1888)
  - Horrie Brain, Australian rules footballer (b. 1885)
  - Henry Bray, Australian rules footballer (b. 1891)

- Gen. Sir Dallas Brooks, British military commander, Governor of Victoria, Australia (b. 1896)
- March 23
  - Peggy Allenby, American silent film, television, and radio actress (b. 1901)
  - August Bach, East German politician (b. 1897)
  - Bertil Bothén, Swedish sailor, competitor at the 1912 Summer Olympics (b. 1892)
- March 24
  - Carl Becker, German Wehrmacht general during World War II (b. 1895)
  - Joseph Leonard Burley, Australian rules football executive (b. 1878)
  - Albert Evans, English footballer and manager (b. 1874)
  - Frederic Foley, American urologist (b. 1891)
- March 25
  - G.R. Blanco White, English judge (b. 1883)
  - Pravir Chandra Bhanj Deo, Maharajah of Bastar state (b. 1929)
- March 26
  - Wilhelm Engel Bredal, Norwegian politician, Member of Parliament (b. 1907)
  - Morris Doob, American sports shooter, competed at the 1936 Summer Olympics (b. 1907)
- March 27
  - Sir Archer Baldwin, British Conservative Party Member of Parliament (b. 1883)
  - Pannalal Bhattacharya, Bengali singer
  - Jan Čarek, Czech writer (b. 1898)
  - Helen Menken, American actress (b. 1901)

- March 28
  - Roy Bell, New Zealand-Australian ornithologist (b. 1882)
  - William W. Church, American football coach (b. 1874)
  - Toni Edgar-Bruce, British actress (b. 1892)
  - Buntarō Futagawa, Japanese film director (b. 1899)
- March 29 – Alfred Edwin Brain Jr., English-born American musician (b. 1885)
- March 30
  - Frederick Gordon Bradley, Canadian and Newfoundland politician, member of the Canadian House of Commons and Canadian Senate, Secretary of State for Canada (b. 1886)
  - Jelly d'Arányi, Hungarian violinist (b. 1893)
  - Erwin Piscator, German theater director (b. 1893)
- March 31
  - Grady Adkins, nicknamed "Butcher Boy", American professional baseball player (*Chicago White Sox*) (b. 1897)
  - Fortunato Calcagno, Italian politician, member of the Chamber of Deputies (b. 1900)
  - William David Doherty, English rugby player and hospital administrator (b. 1893)

April

Evelyn Waugh

- April 1
    - Karl Adam, German Catholic theologian (b. 1876)
    - Arnold Franz Brasz, American artist (b. 1888)
    - Sollie Cohen, American football player (b. 1907)
    - Dimitar Dimov, Bulgarian writer (b. 1909)
    - James G. Ellis, American musician and composer (b. 1880)
    - Flann O'Brien, Irish humorist (b. 1911)
- April 2
    - Charles Brown, New Zealand rugby player (b. 1887)
    - C. S. Forester, English author (b. 1899)
- April 3
    - Russel Crouse, American playwright and librettist (b. 1893)
    - Rocco DiSiglio, American boxer and mobster (b. 1939)
    - Battista Farina, Italian car designer (b. 1893)
- April 4
    - Bernard Adeney, English painter and textile designer (b. 1878)

- Georges de Crequi-Montfort, French sport shooter, competed in 1912 Olympics and 1924 Olympics (b. 1877)
  - Jimmy Daywalt, American race car driver (b. 1924)
  - Maurie De Araugo, Australian rules footballer (b. 1902)
- April 5
  - Clarence Owen Cooper, Canadian politician, member of the Canadian House of Commons (b. 1899)
  - Harold Costley-White, English Anglican priest (b. 1878)
  - Sam Dodge, American baseball player (b. 1889)
  - Ragnar Ekberg, Swedish athlete, competed in the 1908 and 1912 Summer Olympics (b. 1886)
- April 6
  - Père Azaïs, French missionary and archeologist (b. 1870)
  - Emil Brunner, Swiss Reformed theologian (b. 1889)
  - Harold Cotton, Australian cricketer (b. 1914)
  - Hans Engen, Norwegian diplomat (b. 1912)
  - Julia Faye, American actress (b. 1893)
  - Edna Flugrath, American actress (b. 1893)
- April 7
  - Fred G. Aandahl, American politician, governor of North Dakota (1945–1951), member of U.S. House of Representative (1951–1953) (b. 1897)
  - Harry Cator, English recipient of the Victoria Cross (b. 1894)
  - George Cornelius, Australian rules footballer (b. 1874)
  - Basil Davenport, American writer (b. 1905)
  - Bert Dingley, American race car driver (b. 1885)

- April 8 – Carl Schurz Vrooman, Assistant United States Secretary of Agriculture (b. 1872)
- April 9
  - Ralph M. Brown, American politician and judge, speaker of the California State Assembly (b. 1908)
  - Barry Butler, English footballer (b. 1934)
- April 10
  - Heinz Barwich, German nuclear physicist, worked on the Soviet atom bomb program (b. 1911)
  - Evelyn Waugh, English author (b. 1903)
- April 11
  - A. B. Campbell, British naval officer and radio personality (b. 1881)
  - Roman Dzeneladze, Soviet wrestler, competed in the 1956 Summer Olympics (b. 1933)
  - Asmund Enger, Norwegian sports shooter, competed in the 1908 Summer Olympics (b. 1881)
  - Rufus Fitzgerald, American academic administrator, Chancellor of the University of Pittsburgh (b. 1890)
- April 12
  - Milislav Demerec, Austria-Hungary-born American scientist (b. 1895)
  - Sir Waithilingam Duraiswamy, Ceylonese politician, speaker of the State Council of Ceylon (b. 1874)
- April 13
  - Abdul Salam Arif, Iraqi military office and statesman, President of the Republic (b. 1921)
  - Bert Avery, New Zealand rugby league player (b. 1895)
  - Clellan Card, American radio personality (b. 1903)
  - Carlo Carrà, Italian painter (b. 1881)

- Georges Duhamel, French author (b. 1884)
- Lionel Edwards, British artist (b. 1878)
- Billy Fitchford, English footballer and cricketer (b. 1892)
- William S. Flynn, American politician, Governor of Rhode Island (b. 1885)
- April 14
  - John L. Barkley, United States Army Medal of Honor recipient of World War I (b. 1895)
  - Theodore William Chaundy, English mathematician (b. 1889)
- April 15
  - Habibullah Bahar Chowdhury, Pakistani writer and politician, Health Minister of East Pakistan (b. 1906)
  - Joseph Crehan, American actor (b. 1883)
  - Rina De Liguoro, Italian actress (b. 1892)
- April 16
  - Nandalal Bose, Indian painter (b. 1882)
  - Otto Buchinger, German physician (b. 1878)
  - Stafford Cassell, American football coach (b. 1909)
- April 17 – Christiane Delyne, American-born French actress (b. 1902)
- April 18
  - Ernest Bacon, British wrestler, competed in the 1924 Summer Olympics (b. 1893)
  - Maginel Wright Enright, American children's book illustrator (b. 1881)
  - Edward Fitzgerald, American ice hockey player, competed in the 1920 Olympics (b. 1891)
- April 19

- Gösta Åsbrink, Swedish gymnast and modern pentathlete; Olympic athlete: gold medal in the 1908 Summer Olympics, silver medal in the 1912 Summer Olympics (b. 1881)
- Jack Cock, English footballer (b. 1893)
- Brigadier Sir Neil Hamilton Fairley, Australian physician and army officer (b. 1891)
- Javier Solís, Mexican singer (b. 1931)
- April 20
  - Rufus Cole, American doctor (b. 1872)
  - Earle Cook, Canadian politician, member of the Legislative Assembly of Alberta (b. 1881)
  - Prince Frederick of Prussia, German-born British aristocrat, Grandson of the last Kaiser (b. 1911)
- April 21
  - Sepp Dietrich, Nazi German military leader (b. 1892)
  - Archibald Montgomerie, 17th Earl of Eglinton, Scottish nobleman (b. 1914)
- April 22
  - Aslaug Blytt, Norwegian art historian, museum manager, politician (b. 1899)
  - Lou Finney, American baseball player (b. 1910)
- April 23
  - Naima Akef, Egyptian belly-dancer and actress (b. 1929)
  - Heinrich Dollwetzel, East German Major General (b. 1912)
  - George Ohsawa, Japanese diet founder (b. 1893)
- April 24

- Melecio Arranz, Filipino politician; member of the Senate (b. 1888)
- Simon Chikovani, Georgian poet and Soviet politician, deputy to the Supreme Soviet (b. 1902)
- J. Morris Foster, American actor (b. 1881)
- April 25 – Art Decatur, American baseball player (b. 1894)
- April 26
  - Earnest Sevier Cox, American Methodist preacher and political activist (b. 1880)
  - Bill Everson, Welsh rugby player (b. 1906)
  - Roberto Faz, Cuban singer (b. 1914)
  - Tom Florie, American soccer player (b. 1897)
- April 27 – Kenzō Futaki, Japanese doctor (b. 1873)
- April 28 – Joseph Birds, English footballer (b. 1887)
- April 29
  - Rolf Bergersen, Norwegian sport shooter, world champion and Olympic competitor (b. 1906)
  - Earle D. Chesney, American cartoonist (b. 1900)
  - William Eccles, British physicist and radio pioneer (b. 1875)
  - Catherine Fonteney, French actress (b. 1879)
  - Hugo Friend, Austro-Hungarian-born American jurist (b. 1882)
  - Eugene O'Brien, American actor (b. 1880)
- April 30
  - Everett Case, American basketball coach (b. 1900)
  - Richard Fariña, American writer and folksinger (b. 1937)

May

- May 1
  - Albert Arnal, Valencian pilotari (b. 1913)
  - Lee Tung Foo, American actor (b. 1875)
- May 2
  - Bill Amery, Australian rules footballer (b. 1894)
  - Bernice Fisher, American civil rights activist (b. 1916)
  - Agostinho Fortes Filho, Brazilian footballer (b. 1901)
- May 3
  - Alan Don, English Anglican priest, Dean of Westminster during Elizabeth II's coronation (b. 1885)
  - John Gaddy, American baseball player (b. 1914)
- May 4
  - Mick Anthony, Australian rules footballer (b. 1894)
  - Timothy Bevington, English and Canadian cricketer (b. 1881)
  - Wojciech Brydziński, Polish actor (b. 1877)
  - Bob Elliott, American baseball player (b. 1916)
- May 7
  - Lucy Grant Cannon, American religious leader (b. 1880)
  - Hamilton Corbett, American football player (b. 1888)
  - Leonard Deadwyler, American killed by police (b. c. 1941)
  - Carlos Luis Fallas, Costa Rican writer (b. 1909)
- May 8
  - Stefan Anderson, Swedish industrialist, journalist and watchmaker (b. 1878)

- Elisha T. Barrett, American politician from New York, member of the New York State Assembly and New York State Senate (b. 1902)
- Harry Anson Finney, American professor of accounting (b. 1886)
- Erich Pommer, German film producer (b. 1889)
- May 9
  - Joseph Sterling Bridwell, American oilman (b. 1885)
  - Flame Delhi, American baseball player (b. 1892)
- May 10 – Erich Engel, German film and theatre director (b. 1891)
- May 11
  - Hilary A. Bush, American politician, Lieutenant Governor of Missouri (b. 1905)
  - Sir Herbert Butcher, 1st Baronet, English politician, MP (b. 1901)
  - John James Carrick, American-born Canadian politician, member of the House of Commons (b. 1873)
  - Henry S. Caulfield, American politician, Governor of Missouri (b. 1873)
  - Alfred Wintle, British army officer and eccentric (b. 1897)
- May 12
  - Stephen Campbell, Guyanese politician, MP (b. 1897)
  - Bruce Eddis, English cricketer (b. 1883)
- May 13 – Henrik Adam Due, American-born Norwegian violinist (b. 1891)
- May 14
  - Joseph Williams Armstrong, English footballer (b. 1892)
  - Tom Connolly, American baseball player (b. 1892)

- o Irv Constantine, American football player (b. 1907)
- May 15
  - o Kathryn Forbes, American writer (b. 1908)
  - o Maximiliano Hernández Martínez, Salvadorian military dictator (assassinated) (b. 1882)
  - o Titien Sumarni, Indonesian actress (b. 1932)
- May 16
  - o Adm. William Carr, English-born Australian admiral (b. 1883)
  - o Eddie Casey, American football player and coach (b. 1894)
  - o Gen. Merritt B. Curtis, American brigadier general and politician (b. 1892)
- May 17
  - o Vahram Alazan, Soviet Armenian poet, writer and public activist, the First Secretary of the Writers Union of Armenia from 1933 to 1936 (b. 1903)
  - o Deng Tuo, Chinese writer (b. *c.* 1911)
- May 18
  - o Paul Althaus, German Lutheran theologian (b. 1888)
  - o Punk Berryman, American football player and coach (b. 1892)
  - o Paul Joseph Chartier, Canadian would-be bomber of the House of Commons (b. 1921)
- May 20
  - o Hester Adrian, Baroness Adrian, British mental health worker (b. 1899)
  - o Carlos Arruza, nicknamed "El Ciclón" ("the cyclone"), Mexican bullfighter (b. 1920)
- May 21 – Pat O'Malley, American actor (b. 1890)

- May 22
  - John Byers, American architect (b. 1875)
  - William Dickson, English-born Australian politician (b. 1893)
  - Tom Goddard, English cricketer (b. 1900)
- May 23
  - Charles Brand, American politician, U.S. Representative from Ohio (b. 1871)
  - Sam Cooke, Australian rules footballer (b. 1883)
  - Hubert Creekmore, American poet and author (b. 1907)
  - Louis-Charles Damais, French Orientalist (b. 1911)
  - Demchugdongrub, Mongolian politician (b. 1902)
- May 24
  - Henri Barbé, French Communist and collaborator with Nazi Germany (b. 1902)
  - Jim Barnes, English golf champion (b. 1886)
  - Pierre de Lagarde Boal, American diplomat, U.S. Ambassador to Nicaragua and to Bolivia (b. 1895)
  - Alexandru Cazaban, Romanian writer (b. 1872)
  - Sir Herbert Dowbiggin, British Inspector General of Police of Ceylon (b. 1880)
  - Emil Fahrenkamp, German architect (b. 1885)
  - Niaz Fatehpuri, Indian-born Pakistani writer (b. 1884)
  - Ove Frederiksen, Danish tennis player, competed at the 1912 Summer Olympics (b. 1884)
- May 25
  - William Acorn, Canadian automobile dealer and politician; member of the Legislative Assembly of Prince Edward Island (b. 1915)

- André Baugé, French opera and operetta singer and film actor (b. 1893)
- Vernon Sturdee, Australian general (b. 1890)
- May 26
  - Don Castle, American actor (b. 1917)
  - Elizabeth Dilling, American anti-communist and antisemitic activist (b. 1894)
- May 27 – Vic Buchanan, Australian rules footballer (b. 1899)
- May 28 – Simon Ericsson, Swedish rower, competed in the 1912 Summer Olympics (b. 1886)
- May 29 – James Woolf, British film producer (b. 1919)
- May 30
  - Wäinö Aaltonen, Finnish artist and sculptor (b. 1894)
  - Vladimir Alafuzov, Soviet admiral (b. 1901)
  - Oscar Walter Cisek, Romanian writer (b. 1897)
- May 31 – Gen. William H. Blanchard, United States Air Force general (b. 1916)

June

- June 1
  - Herbert Bowmer, English cricketer (b. 1891)
  - Cécile Butticaz, Swiss engineer (b. 1884)
  - Dick Cox, American baseball player (b. 1897)
  - Papa Jack Laine, American jazz musician (b. 1873)
- June 2
  - François Ayoub, Syrian Archbishop of Aleppo and Cyprus (b. 1899)
  - Arthur P. Bedou, American photographer (b. 1882)
  - Joe Casey, American baseball player (b. 1887)

- June 3
  - Connie Brown, Canadian hockey player (b. 1917)
  - Alice Calhoun, American actress (b. 1900)
  - Dario Canas, Portuguese sports shooter, Olympic competitor at 1920 Summer Olympics and 1924 Summer Olympics (b. 1884)
  - Reuben Swinburne Clymer, American occultist (b. 1878)
- June 4
  - Chang Myon, South Korean statesman, Vice President, Prime Minister (b. 1899)
  - Arthur C. Cope, American organic chemist (b. 1909)
  - Teddy Davis, American boxer (b. 1923)
- June 5 – Edward Arthur Carr, British colonial administrator of Nigeria (b. 1903)
- June 6
  - Sir Elias Wynne Cemlyn-Jones, Welsh politician (b. 1888)
  - Ethel Clayton, American actress (b. 1882)
- June 7
  - Jean Arp, Alsatian sculptor, painter, and poet (b. 1887)
  - Norman Baillie-Stewart, British army officer known as "The Officer in the Tower" when he was imprisoned in the Tower of London for collaboration with Nazi Germany in World War II (b. 1909)
  - John Adam Day, British politician (b. 1901)
- June 8
  - Jim Dixon, American football player (b. 1904)
  - Anton Melik, Slovenian geographer (b. 1890)
- June 9

- o Max Friz, German design engineer (b. 1883)
- o Sherry Edmundson Fry, American sculptor (b. 1879)
- June 10
  - o Joseph Biondo, Italian-born American organized crime figure (b. 1897)
  - o Felice Carena, Italian painter (b. 1879)
  - o Gunnar Ekstrand, Swedish diver, competed in the 1912 and 1920 Summer Olympics (b. 1892)
  - o Wally Fraser, Australian rules footballer (b. 1897)
- June 11
  - o Alfred Berger, Austrian pair skater, Olympic gold medalist in 1924 (b. 1894)
  - o Thomas Hardie Chalmers, American opera singer and actor (b. 1884)
  - o Rube Currie, American baseball player (b. 1898)
  - o Timothy Curtis, English cricketer (b. 1882)
  - o Jimmy Davies, American race car driver (b. 1929)
  - o Wallace Ford, English-born American actor (b. 1898)
- June 12 – Hermann Scherchen, Austrian conductor (b. 1891)
- June 13 – Pierre Chaumié, French politician, member of the French Senate (b. 1880)
- June 14
  - o Walther Bacmeister, German jurist and ornithologist (b. 1873)
  - o Cub Buck, American football player and coach and college athletics administrator (b. 1892)
  - o Parnaoz Chikviladze, Soviet judoka, bronze medalist at the 1964 Summer Olympics (b. 1941)
  - o Henny Dons, Norwegian educator and missionary (b. 1874)

- June 15 – Robert G. Fowler, American aviation pioneer (b. 1884)
- June 16
  - Dantès Bellegarde, Haitian diplomat (b. 1877)
  - Lew Brice, American dancer and comedian (b. 1893)
- June 17
  - Betty Baxter Anderson, American author (b. 1908)
  - Hans Christern, German officer during World War II (b. 1900)
  - Luby DiMeolo, American football player and coach (b. 1903)
- June 18 – German Galynin, Soviet composer (b. 1922)
- June 19
  - Sydney Allard, British racing motorist and founder of the Allard car company (b. 1910)
  - Chalmers Clifton, American conductor and composer (b. 1889)
  - Ed Wynn, American actor (b. 1886)
- June 20
  - Capt. Sir Malcolm Bullock, 1st Baronet, British soldier, politician, and nobleman, MP (b. 1890)
  - Wilhelm Busch, German pastor and anti-Nazi (b. 1897)
  - Cheng Bugao, Chinese film director (b. 1898)
  - John Hubbard, 3rd Baron Addington, British aristocrat (b. 1883)
  - Georges Lemaître, Belgian priest and astrophysicist (b. 1894)
- June 21 – Reginald Calvert, British pirate radio station operator (b. 1928)
- June 22

- o Roger Blunt, English-born New Zealand cricketer (b. 1900)
- o E. Yale Dawson, American botanist (b. 1918)
- o Warren S. Eaton, American aviation pioneer (b. 1891)
- June 23
  - o Paul Cain, American author (b. 1902)
  - o Ted Corday, Canadian-born American television executive (b. 1908)
  - o Louis C. Cramton, American politician, United States Representative from Michigan (b. 1875)
- June 24
  - o Edward Allworth, American officer in the United States Army during World War I (*Medal of Honor*) (b. 1895)
  - o Eric Crankshaw, English cricketer (b. 1885)
  - o Mick Dunn, Australian rules footballer (b. 1898)
  - o Otto-Wilhelm Förster, German general during World War II (b. 1885)
- June 25
  - o Ughetto Bertucci, Italian actor (b. 1907)
  - o F. Henri Klickmann, American composer (b. 1885)
- June 26 – François Dupré, French hotelier, art collector, racehorse owner/breeder (b. 1888)
- June 28
  - o Kenneth Miller Adams, American artist (b. 1897)
  - o Gleason Archer, Sr., founder and first president of Suffolk University and Suffolk Law School in Boston, Massachusetts (b. 1880)
  - o Frances Maule Bjorkman, American suffragist (b. 1879)
- June 29 – Lewis Bedford, English footballer (b. 1899)
- June 30

- Margery Allingham, English writer of detective fiction (b. 1904)
- Loretta Bayliss, New Zealand cricketer (b. 1939)
- Mordaunt Doll, English cricketer (b. 1888)
- Giuseppe Farina, Italian race car driver (b. 1906)
- Ernest Fawcus, English cricketer (b. 1895)

July

Montgomery Clift

- July 1
  - Wiri Baker, New Zealand cricketer (b. 1892)
  - Pauline Boty, British artist (b. 1938)
  - Johnny Bryan, American football player and coach (b. 1897)
  - Georg Ehrlich, Austrian-born British sculptor (b. 1897)
  - Bill Galvin, Australian politician, member of the Victorian Legislative Assembly (b. 1903)
- July 2
  - Jan Brzechwa, Polish poet (b. 1900)
  - Minnie D. Craig, American politician, Speaker of the North Dakota House of Representatives (b. 1883)

- July 3
  - Kees Boeke, Dutch pacifist and tax resister (b. 1884)
  - Robert Cochrane, English occultist (b. 1931)
  - Deems Taylor, American composer (b. 1885)
- July 4
  - Dorothy Aldis, American children's author and poet (b. 1896)
  - Louis Couffignal, French mathematician (b. 1902)
  - Georges Dumont, Canadian politician, member of the Legislative Assembly of New Brunswick (b. 1898)
- July 5
  - Robin Sutcliffe Allan, New Zealand geologist and university professor (b. 1900)
  - Edward Pierrepont Beckwith, American scientist (b. 1877)
  - Vinson Allen Collins, American politician, member of the Texas Senate (b. 1867)
  - Pete Fox, American baseball player (b. 1909)
  - George de Hevesy, Hungarian chemist, Nobel Prize laureate (b. 1885)
- July 6
  - Harold Breen, Australian public servant (b. 1893)
  - Sad Sam Jones, American baseball player (b. 1892)
  - Anne Nagel, American actress (b. 1915)
- July 7
  - Yoshishige Abe, Japanese philosopher, educator, and statesman in Shōwa period Japan; Minister of Education (b. 1883)
  - Carmelita Geraghty, American actress (b. 1901)
- July 8

- Dick Christy, American football player (b. 1935)
- Herbert Elphinstone, Australian cricket umpire (b. 1905)
- Horst Fischer, German war criminal, last person guillotined in Germany (b. 1912)
- July 9 – Sir John Lindsay Dashwood, 10th Baronet, English aristocrat (b. 1896)
- July 10
  - Raphaël Etifier, French politician, member of the French senate (b. 1889)
  - G'afur G'ulom, Uzbek writer (b. 1903)
- July 11
  - Billy Butler, English footballer (b. 1900)
  - Delmore Schwartz, American poet (b. 1913)
- July 12
  - Vera Franceschi, American pianist (b. 1926)
  - D. T. Suzuki, Japanese philosopher (b. 1870)
- July 13
  - Genica Athanasiou, Romanian-French actress (b. 1897)
  - Princess Beatrice of Saxe-Coburg and Gotha, member of the British Royal Family, granddaughter of Queen Victoria (b. 1884)
- July 14 – Julie Manet, French painter (b. 1878)
- July 15
  - Seyfi Arkan, Turkish architect (b. 1903)
  - Francis Agar-Robartes, 7th Viscount Clifden, British politician (b. 1883)
  - Wilhelm Cornides, Wehrmacht sergeant in World War II, diarist (b. 1920)
- July 16

- o Arthur Adamson, Australian rules football player (b. 1882)
- o Richard Craig, Canadian politician, member of the Legislative Assembly of Manitoba (b. 1877)
- o Agnes Dollan, Scottish suffragist and politician (b. 1887)
- o Bernhard Schweitzer, German archaeologist (b. 1892)
- July 17
  - o August Baeyens, Belgian violist and composer (b. 1895)
  - o Charles Creed, French-born British fashion designer (b. 1909)
  - o Nils Dahl, Norwegian runner, competed at the 1908 and 1912 Olympics (b. 1882)
  - o Albert Freethy, Welsh rugby referee and cricketer (b. 1885)
- July 18 – Bobby Fuller, American musician (b. 1942)
- July 19
  - o Walter Aitkenhead, Scottish footballer (b. 1887)
  - o Mary Jobe Akeley, American explorer and author (b. 1878)
  - o Joaquín Albareda y Ramoneda, Spanish Roman Catholic Cardinal (b. 1892)
  - o Maxine Albro, American painter, muralist, lithographer, mosaic artist, and sculptor (b. 1903)
- July 20
  - o Elizabeth Amsden, American operatic soprano and actress (b. 1881)
  - o Alexander Bazhbeuk-Melikyan, Soviet artist, graphic designer and sculptor (b. 1891)

- Anne Beffort, Luxembourg educator and author (b. 1880)
- Julien Carette, French actor (b. 1897)
- July 21
  - Francis Stewart Briggs, Australian aviator (b. 1897)
  - Francesco Paolo Cantelli, Italian mathematician (b. 1875)
  - Philipp Frank, Austrian-born American scientist and philosopher (b. 1884)
  - John French, English photographer (b. 1907)
- July 22
  - Vladimir Abrikosov, Russian Catholic priest of the Byzantine rite (b. 1880)
  - Lauro Ayestarán, Uruguayan musicologist (b. 1913)
  - Berend Carp, Dutch sailor, competed at the 1920 Summer Olympics (b. 1901)
  - Harriet Daggett, American law professor (b. 1891)
  - Frank Delahanty, American baseball player (b. 1882)
- July 23
  - Kurt Albrecht, German military officer during World War II (b. 1895)
  - Margaret Bennell, English educator (b. 1893)
  - Vito R. Bertoldo, United States Army soldier, Medal of Honor recipient (b. 1916)
  - Douglass Montgomery, American actor (b. 1907)
- July 24
  - Aftimios Ofiesh, American Orthodox bishop (b. 1880)
  - George Brook, English cricketer (b. 1888)
  - Montgomery Clift, American actor (b. 1920)
  - Harry Cobe, American racecar driver (b. 1885)

- July 25
  - Harold Conradi, Australian rules footballer (b. 1894)
  - Francis Edward Faragoh, Austria-Hungary-born American screenwriter (b. 1898)
  - Frank O'Hara, American poet (b. 1926)
- July 26
  - Gladstone Adams, British politician; Chairman of Whitley Bay Urban District Council (b. 1880)
  - Brenda Sue Brown, American murder victim (b. 1955)
  - Jean-Edouard de Castella, Australian-born Swiss artist (b. 1881)
  - Augustine Duffy, Canadian politician, member of the Newfoundland House of Assembly (b. 1905)
- July 27 – Edward Carey Francis, English mathematician and Christian missionary to Kenya (b. 1897)
- July 28
  - Josef von Báky, Hungarian filmmaker (b. 1902)
  - Judd Conlon, American vocal arranger and conductor (b. 1910)
  - Hal Dixon, American baseball umpire (b. 1920)
- July 29
  - Maj. Gen. Johnson Aguiyi-Ironsi, Nigerian military figure and Head of State of Nigeria (b. 1924)
  - Russell Clark, New Zealand artist (b. 1905)
  - Edward Gordon Craig, English theatre practitioner (b. 1872)
  - Jerry Dennerlein, American football player (b. 1915)
  - Harold Egan, Australian rules footballer (b. 1884)
  - Adekunle Fajuyi, Nigerian soldier, first military governor of the Western Region, Nigeria (b. 1926)

- Billy Fogg, English footballer (b. 1903)
- July 30
  - Hazel Abel, American teacher and politician; United States Senator (b. 1888)
  - George Ford, Australian politician, member of the New South Wales Legislative Council (b. 1907)
  - Gen. Otto Fretter-Pico, German general during World War II (b. 1893)
  - Sir Donald Gainer, British diplomat, Ambassador to Venezuela, Brazil, and Poland (b. 1891)
- July 31
  - Andrej Bagar, Slovak film actor (b. 1900)
  - Chester R. Davis, American businessman, Assistant Secretary of the Army (b. 1896)
  - Alexander von Falkenhausen, German general (b. 1878)
  - Bud Powell, American jazz pianist (b. 1924)

August

Lenny Bruce

- August 2
  - Rudolf Antonín Dvorský, Czech bandleader (b. 1899)
  - Jacques Fouques-Duparc, French diplomat (b. 1897)
- August 3
  - Earl Blackburn, American baseball player (b. 1892)

- ○ Lenny Bruce, American comedian (b. 1925)
- ○ John Cockle, English-born Australian politician, member of the Australian House of Representatives (b. 1908)
- August 4
  - ○ Betty Arlen, American actress (b. 1909)
  - ○ Pug Cavet, American baseball player (b. 1889)
- August 5
  - ○ Bian Zhongyun, Chinese educator, first victim of the Cultural Revolution (b. 1916)
  - ○ John Cairney, New Zealand anatomist (b. 1898)
  - ○ Nobby Clark, Canadian ice hockey player (b. 1897)
  - ○ Austin Diamond, English-born Australian cricketer (b. 1874)
- August 6
  - ○ Edmond L. DePatie, American film industry executive (b. 1900)
  - ○ Cordwainer Smith, American author (b. 1913)
- August 7 – Samuel J. Battle, American police officer, first African-American police officer in New York City (b. 1883)
- August 8
  - ○ Herman Bartlett, Australian rules footballer (b. 1892)
  - ○ Teddy Billington, American racing cyclist, multiple medalist at the 1904 Olympic games (b. 1882)
  - ○ Ed "Strangler" Lewis, professional wrestler (b. 1891)
- August 9
  - ○ Axel Alfredsson, Swedish footballer, Olympic competitor (*1924*) (b. 1902)
  - ○ Lee Bowers, American witness to the assassination of John F. Kennedy (b. 1925)

- Henri Fescourt, French film director (b. 1880)
- August 10
    - J. C. Bloem, Dutch poet and writer (b. 1887)
    - Arthur Creber, British cricketer (b. 1909)
    - Chuck Dressen, American baseball player and manager (b. 1894)
    - James French, American murderer (b. *c.* 1936)
- August 11 – Ettore Bellotto, Italian gymnast, member of the gold-medal winning team at the 1920 Summer Olympics (b. 1895)
- August 12
    - Artur Alliksaar, Estonian poet (b. 1923)
    - J. H. Conradie, South African politician and judge, Speaker of the National Assembly (b. 1897)
- August 13
    - Frank Chester, Canadian politician, member of the Legislative Assembly of Manitoba (b. 1901)
    - Laura Gardin Fraser, American sculptor (b. 1889)
- August 14 – Raymond Duncan, American writer and philosopher (b. 1874)
- August 15
    - George Burns, American baseball player (b. 1889)
    - Chris Cameron, Australian rules footballer (b. 1894)
    - Jules Dubois, American reporter (b. 1910)
    - Rafael Frontaura, Chilean actor (b. 1896)
    - Jan Kiepura, Polish tenor and actor (b. 1902)
    - Seena Owen, American actress (b. 1894)
- August 17
    - Bill Allington, American minor league baseball player and manager (b. 1903)

- o Jean-Yves Bigras, Canadian film director and editor (b. 1919)
- o Rolf Billberg, Swedish alto saxophone player (b. 1930)
- August 19
  - o Fritz Bleyl, German painter (b. 1880)
  - o Carlo Capra, Italian footballer (b. 1889)
  - o Roy Crick, Australian politician, member of the Victorian Legislative Assembly (b. 1904)
  - o Jeanne de Casalis, Basutoland-born British actress (b. 1897)
- August 20
  - o Arthur Colvin, Australian doctor and politician, member of the New South Wales Legislative Council (b. 1884)
  - o Austin Diamond, American politician (b. 1874)
  - o Urban Huttleston Broughton, 1st Baron Fairhaven, American-born British nobleman (b. 1896)
- August 21
  - o Terry Beddard, British fencer; Olympic competitor (1936 and 1948) (b. 1901)
  - o Jack Bisset, Australian rules footballer (b. 1900)
  - o Martin Dooling, American soccer player, bronze medalist at the 1904 Summer Olympics (b. 1886)
- August 22
  - o Gunnar Aaby, Danish soccer player (b. 1895)
  - o Benjamin C. Dawkins, Sr., American judge (b. 1881)
- August 23 – Francis X. Bushman, American actor (b. 1883)
- August 24
  - o Malfred Bergseth, Norwegian trade unionist (b. 1895)

- o Tadeusz Bór-Komorowski, Polish general and statesman (b. 1895)
  - o Wheezer Dell, American baseball player (b. 1886)
  - o Sam Faubus, American politician (b. 1887)
- August 25
  - o James Bagshaw, English football player (*Derby County*) (b. 1885)
  - o Lance Comfort, English film director (b. 1908)
  - o Sir John Dwyer, Australian jurist, Chief Justice and Lieutenant Governor of Western Australia (b. 1879)
- August 26
  - o Nils Asheim, Norwegian Liberal Party politician (b. 1895)
  - o Art Baker, American actor (b. 1898)
  - o Edmund Blampied, Jersey artist (b. 1886)
  - o Norm Davis, Australian rules footballer (b. 1904)
  - o Robert Dehler, Canadian-born Bermudan Roman Catholic bishop (b. 1889)
- August 27
  - o Mads Clausen, Danish industrialist (b. 1905)
  - o John Cournos, Russian-born American and British writer (b. 1881)
- August 28
  - o Waldemar Carlsen, Norwegian writer, newspaper editor, and politician (b. 1880)
  - o Andrew Edmiston, Jr., American politician, United States Representative from West Virginia (b. 1892)
- August 29
  - o Princess Augusta Victoria of Hohenzollern, German princess (b. 1890)

- Emil Burri, German playwright and screenwriter (b. 1902)
- Fritz Max Cahén, German anti-Nazi (b. 1891)
- Elmer Talmadge Clark, American writer and church executive (b. 1886)
- Al DeVormer, American baseball player (b. 1891)
- Joseph Egger, Austrian actor (b. 1889)
- August 30
  - John Campbell, Australian rugby player (b. 1889)
  - Martin W. Clement, American railroad executive (b. 1881)
- August 31
  - Joyce Allan, Australian conchologist (b. 1896)
  - Alexis Caron, Canadian politician, member of the House of Commons (b. 1899)

September

- September 1
  - Karl Bergelt, German Navy officer during World War II (b. 1902)
  - Mabel Capper, British suffragist (b. 1888)
- September 2 – George Bolt, Australian rules footballer (b. 1899)
- September 3
  - Constantin Bakaleinikoff, Russian-born American composer (b. 1896)
  - Dick Barwegan, American professional football player (b. 1921)
  - Sir Robert Bristow, English engineer (b. 1880)

- Chen Mengjia, Chinese archaeologist (b. 1911)
- Wesley Dennis, American illustrator (b. 1903)
- Fu Lei, Chinese translator and art critic (b. 1908)
- September 4
  - Bernard Atkinson, English cricketer (b. 1900)
  - August Aimé Balkema, Dutch book trader (b. 1906)
  - Herbert Beyer, German paratrooper officer during World War II (b. 1913)
- September 5
  - William Murdoch Buchanan, Canadian politician, member of the Canadian House of Commons (b. 1897)
  - Edward Denman Clarke, Finnish-born British flying ace of World War I (b. 1898)
  - Edward English, English cricketer (b. 1864)
  - Dezső Lauber, Hungarian sportsman and architect (b. 1879)
- September 6
  - Margaret Sanger, American birth control advocate (b. 1879)
  - Hendrik Verwoerd, Dutch-born Prime Minister of South Africa (b. 1901)
- September 7 – Viktor Ader, Estonian footballer (b. 1910)
- September 8 – Walter Friedländer, German-American art historian (b. 1873)
- September 9 – Jack Cobb, American basketball player (b. 1904)
- September 10
  - Blair Cherry, American baseball and football coach (b. 1901)
  - Arthur Cock, Australian rules footballer (b. 1900)

- September 11
  - Arthur Affleck, Australian pilot (b. 1903)
  - Hans von Ahlfen, German General in the Second World War (b. 1897)
  - Charley Aylett, Australian politician (b. 1913)
  - Charlie Cantor, American radio actor (b. 1898)
  - Bill Cramer, American baseball player (b. 1891)
  - C. E. Woolman, American Airlines founder (b. 1889)
- September 12
  - Florence Ellinwood Allen, American judge; the first woman to serve on a state supreme court (Ohio), and one of the first two women to serve as a United States federal judge (b. 1884)
  - Francis Sheed Anderson CB, Scottish businessman, civil servant and Liberal Party politician (b. 1897)
  - Iosif Czako, Romanian footballer (b. 1906)
  - Aketo Nakamura, Japanese general (b. 1889)
- September 13
  - Wiktor Andersson, Swedish film actor (b. 1887)
  - Dora Barton, English actress (b. 1884)
  - Major General Francis William Billado, American military officer and politician, member of the Vermont House of Representatives, Adjutant General of the Vermont National Guard (b. 1907)
  - Clemente Canepari, Italian racing cyclist (b. 1886)
  - John Christoffersen, Danish wrestler, competed at the 1924 Summer Olympics (b. 1898)
  - Ralph Comstock, American baseball player (b. 1890)
  - Alfred Engelsen, Norwegian gymnast and diver, gold medalist at the 1912 Summer Olympics (b. 1893)

- Tomoshige Samejima, Japanese admiral (b. 1889)
- September 14
  - Gertrude Berg, American actress (b. 1899)
  - Alexandre Bioussa, French rugby union player, member of the silver medal-winning French team at the 1924 Summer Olympics (b. 1901)
  - Nikolay Cherkasov, Soviet actor (b. 1903)
  - Arthur Davies, English Anglican priest (b. 1878)
  - Hiram Wesley Evans, American leader of the Ku Klux Klan (b. 1881)
  - Cemal Gürsel, Turkish general and statesman, 4th President of Turkey (b. 1895)
- September 15
  - Frank G. Ashbrook, American mammalogist (b. 1892)
  - Leonard Brockington, Welsh-born Canadian civil servant, first president of the Canadian Broadcasting Corporation (b. 1888)
- September 16
  - Anandashram Swami, Indian ninth guru and the Head of the community of the Chitrapur Saraswats (b. 1902)
  - Lawrence Joseph Bader, American whose disappearance and later reappearance caused controversy (b. 1926)
- September 17
  - Selmer Berg, Canadian politician, member of the Legislative Assembly of Alberta (b. 1886)
  - Mário Filho, Brazilian journalist and writer (b. 1908)
  - Fritz Wunderlich, German tenor (b. 1930)
- September 18
  - Ian Bedford, English cricketer (b. 1930)

- Gen. Horace H. Fuller, American general during World War II (b. 1886)
- September 19
  - José de Jesús Angulo del Valle y Navarro, Mexican Roman Catholic bishop (b. 1888)
  - Adrien Borel, French psychiatrist (b. 1886)
  - Albert van der Sandt Centlivres, South African jurist, Chief Justice of South Africa (b. 1887)
  - Albert Divo, French race car driver (b. 1895)
  - Gen. Vladimir Grigoryevich Fyodorov, Soviet weapons designer and general during World War II (b. 1874)
- September 20
  - William Baragwanath, Australian surveyor and geologist (b. 1878)
  - Pierre E. Belliveau, Canadian politician, member of the Nova Scotia House of Assembly (b. 1896)
  - Fritz Delius, German actor (b. 1890)
  - Hubert L. Eaton, American businessman (b. 1881)
- September 21 – Paul Reynaud, French politician, former Prime Minister (b. 1878)
- September 22
  - Valentin Bulgakov, Russian biographer (b. 1886)
  - James A. Chapman, American oilman (b. 1881)
  - Jules Furthman, American screenwriter (b. 1888)
- September 23 – William Beesley VC, English recipient of the Victoria Cross (b. 1895)
- September 24 – Kálmán Blahó, Hungarian sprint canoer, competed at the 1948 Summer Olympics (b. 1920)
- September 25

- o Clifton Cushman, American athlete, silver medalist at the 1960 Summer Olympics (b. 1938)
- o Sir Benjamin Dawson, 1st Baronet, British aristocrat (b. 1878)
- o William Elsey, Australian Anglican priest, Bishop of Kalgoorlie (b. 1880)
- September 26
  - o Aleksandr Anufriyev, Soviet athlete, Olympic athlete (*1952*) (b.1926)
  - o Bill Atkinson, Australian rules footballer (b. 1876)
  - o Jimmy Bridges, English cricketer (b. 1887)
  - o Gus Edson, American cartoonist (b. 1901)
  - o Helen Kane, American singer (b. 1904)
- September 28
  - o André Breton, French poet and writer (b. 1896)
  - o Charles Lawrence Bishop, Canadian journalist and politician, member of the Canadian Senate (b. 1876)
  - o Eric Fleming, American actor (b. 1925)
- September 29 – Zoilo Canavery, Uruguayan-born Argentine footballer (b. 1893)
- September 30 – John Barrett, American football player (b. 1899)

October

Elizabeth Arden

- October 1
  - Michael "Trigger Mike" Coppola, American mobster (b. 1900)
  - Donald S. Day, American reporter and collaborator with Nazi Germany (b. 1895)
  - Cyril Dumpleton, British politician, MP (b. 1897)
- October 2
  - Egmont Arens, American publisher of literature and art, industrial designer, and commercial artist (b. 1889)
  - Jules Boedt, Belgian lawyer and politician (b. 1884)
  - Jumbo Brown, American baseball player (b. 1907)
- October 3
  - George van den Bergh, Dutch law professor and amateur astronomer (b. 1890)
  - Teodors Bergs, Latvian chess master (b. 1902)
  - Raymond Evershed, 1st Baron Evershed, English judge (b. 1899)
- October 4

- Sherman Billingsley, American nightclub owner (the *Stork Club*) (b. 1896)
  - Oscar Cox, American lawyer and judge (b. 1905)
  - Pierre Dufaur de Gavardie, French flying ace of World War I (b. 1890)
- October 5 – Korbinian Aigner, known as Apfelpfarrer ("apple pastor"), German Catholic priest and pomologist (b. 1885)
- October 6
  - Sir George Abbiss OBE, British Chief Constable in the London Metropolitan Police (b. 1884)
  - Sir Alexander Carr-Saunders, English academic, Director of the London School of Economics (b. 1886)
  - Pierre Couderc, French screenwriter and actor (b. 1896)
  - Mitchell Fields, Romanian-born American sculptor (b. 1901)
- October 7
  - Grigoris Asikis, Greek singer and songwriter of urban Greek music (b. 1890)
  - Johnny Kidd, English singer (b. 1935)
  - Smiley Lewis, African-American R&B musician (b. 1913)
- October 8
  - Juan Batlle Planas, Spanish-born Argentine painter (b. 1911)
  - Célestin Freinet, French educational reformer (b. 1896)
- October 9
  - Fedor Astakhov, Soviet Marshal of the aviation (b. 1892)

- William Gage Brady, Jr., American banker, chairman of the National City Bank of New York (b. 1887)
- October 10
  - Melville E. Abrams, American lawyer and politician from New York; member of the NY State Assembly (b. 1912)
  - Abraham Binder, American composer (b. 1895)
  - Kurt Bolender, German SS-man, operated the gas chambers at Sobibór(b. 1912)
  - Colette Bonheur, née Colette Chailler, Canadian singer (b. 1927)
  - Charlotte Cooper, English tennis champion (b. 1870)
  - Robert Desoille, French psychotherapist (b. 1890)
  - Vladimir Dyomin, Soviet footballer and coach (b. 1921)
  - Jack Ferguson, Australian rules footballer (b. 1901)
  - Wilfrid Lawson, English actor (b. 1900)
- October 12 – Venerable Sergio Bernardini, Italian layman beatified by Pope Francis (b. 1882)
- October 13 – Clifton Webb, American actor (b. 1889)
- October 14
  - George Carstairs, Australian rugby player (b. 1900)
  - Arthur Folwell, English-born Australian rugby player (b. 1904)
- October 15
  - Frederick Montague, 1st Baron Amwell CBE, British Labour Party politician (b. 1876)
  - Jon Andrå, Norwegian Labour Party politician (b. 1888)
  - Lee Blair, American jazz musician (b. 1903)
  - Adam Falkenstein, German Assyriologist (b. 1906)
- October 16

- o Arturo Dazzi, Italian artist (b. 1881)
- o George O'Hara, American actor (b. 1899)
- October 17
  - o Dhammalok Mahasthavir, Nepalese Buddhist monk (b. 1890)
  - o Alexander Kulik, Russian cleric (b. 1911)
- October 18
  - o Elizabeth Arden, Canadian-born beautician and cosmetics entrepreneur (b. 1878)
  - o Cyril Briggs, Nevis-born American Communist Party leader (b. 1888)
  - o Joe Chandler, Australian rules footballer (b. 1877)
  - o Honor Crowley, Irish politician, TD (b. 1903)
- October 20
  - o Harry F. Byrd, American politician, Senator from Virginia (b. 1887)
  - o Sir Roy Cameron, Australian pathologist, President of the Royal College of Pathologists (b. 1899)
  - o Charles Catteau, French industrial designer (b. 1880)
  - o Walter Chadwick, English footballer (b. 1903)
  - o Mohamed Fawzi, Egyptian composer and singer (b. 1918)
- October 21
  - o Alfred Cockayne, New Zealand botanist (b. 1880)
  - o Lewis Cohen, Baron Cohen of Brighton, British politician (b. 1897)
- October 22 – Jack Evans, Australian rules footballer (b. 1891)
- October 23
  - o Eugenio Bava, Italian cinematographer (b. 1886)
  - o George Bell, Australian painter (b. 1878)

- ○ Fred Fussell, American baseball player (b. 1895)
- ○ Claire McDowell, silent screen actress (b. 1877)
- October 24
  - ○ Joe Bach, American football player (Notre Dame) and coach (Pittsburgh Steelers) (b. 1901)
  - ○ Hans Dreier, German-born American art director (b. 1885)
  - ○ Leo Friedlander, American sculptor (b. 1888)
- October 25
  - ○ Reginald Crummack, British field hockey player, competed at 1920 Summer Olympics (b. 1887)
  - ○ Floyd MacMillan Davis, American artist (b. 1896)
  - ○ Col. William O. Eareckson, American Air Force officer (b. 1900)
- October 26
  - ○ Katyayanidas Bhattacharya, Indian philosopher (b. 1917)
  - ○ Alma Cogan, English singer (b. 1932)
  - ○ Sir James Coats, 3rd Baronet, British skeleton racer, competed at the 1948 Winter Olympics (b. 1894)
  - ○ Bill Cronin, American baseball player (b. 1902)
- October 27
  - ○ Mush Crawford, American football player (b. 1898)
  - ○ Malcolm Dobie, American-born Canadian politician, Member of the Legislative Assembly of Saskatchewan (b. 1885)
  - ○ Barry Faulkner, American artist (b. 1881)
- October 28

- Nikolai Belyaev, Soviet politician, Secretary of the Central Committee of the Communist Party of the Soviet Union (b. 1903)
- Robert Charpentier, French Olympic cyclist (b. 1916)
- Eugène Hénaff, French trade union leader and member of the French Resistance (b. 1904)
- October 29
  - Wellman Braud, American jazz musician (b. 1891)
  - Thomas Brennan, Australian politician, Victorian MLC (b. 1900)
  - Jocelyn Brooke, English author (b. 1908)
  - Anthony Cavalcante, American politician, United States Representative for Pennsylvania (b. 1897)
- October 30
  - Dick Barrett, American baseball MLB pitcher (b. 1906)
  - John Butt, English cricketer (b. 1892)
  - Rex Cecil, American baseball player (b. 1916)
  - John Drainie, Canadian actor and television presenter (b. 1916)
  - Bill Farnsworth, Australian rugby player (b. 1887)

November

- November 1 – Charles Catterall, South African boxer, silver medal at the 1936 Summer Olympics (b. 1914)
- November 2
  - Sadao Araki, Japanese Army general during World War II (b. 1877)
  - Domenico Cavagnari, Italian admiral, chief of staff of the Italian Royal Navy (b. 1876)

- Peter Debye, Dutch-American chemist working in Nazi Germany, Nobel Prize laureate (b. 1884)
  - Mississippi John Hurt, African-American singer and guitarist (b. 1893)
- November 3
  - Byron Barr, American actor (b. 1917)
  - Fritz Baumgarten, German book illustrator (b. 1883)
  - Streeter Blair, American painter (b. 1888)
  - John T. Cahill, American lawyer (b. 1903)
- November 4
  - Air Chief Marshal Sir Arthur Barratt, British RAF officer, (b. 1891)
  - Gen. Dietrich von Choltitz, Nazi German military governor of Paris in World War II (b. 1894)
- November 6
  - Germaine Dermoz, French actress (b. 1888)
  - Ernst Fabri, Austrian-born Soviet journalist (b. 1891)
  - Hugh Fraser, 1st Baron Fraser of Allander, British nobleman and retailer (b. 1903)
- November 7 – Rube Bressler, American baseball player (b. 1894)
- November 8
  - Frank B. Anderson, American college football, and baseball coach as well as athletic director (b. 1882)
  - Shorty Baker, American jazz trumpeter (b. 1914)
  - André Bloc, French sculptor (b. 1896)
  - Sir Philip Colfox, 1st Baronet, English soldier and politician, MP (b. 1888)
  - Hans Finohr, German actor (b. 1891)

- Bernhard Zondek German-born Israeli gynecologist, developer of first reliable pregnancy test (b. 1891)
- November 9
  - Richard Benz, German historian and writer (b. 1884)
  - Jisaburō Ozawa, Japanese admiral (b. 1886)
- November 10
  - Sir Henry Dalton, English police executive (b. 1891)
  - Eddie Erdelatz, American football player and coach (b. 1913)
- November 12
  - Zeenat Begum, Pakistani singer
  - Donald L. Branson, American racecar driver (b. 1920)
  - Chic Calderwood, Scottish boxer (b. 1937)
  - Shakeb Jalali, Pakistani poet (b. 1934)
- November 13
  - Dick Atkins, American race car driver (b. 1936)
  - Mario Chamlee, American opera singer (b. 1892)
- November 14
  - Peter Baker, British politician, last MP expelled from the House of Commons (b. 1921)
  - Zengo Yoshida, Japanese admiral (b. 1885)
- November 15
  - Billy Dougall, Scottish football player and manager (b. 1895)
  - Aymar Embury II, American architect (b. 1880)
- November 16 – Eric Arbuthnot, South African cricketer (b. 1888)
- November 17
  - Wally Chalmers, Australian rules footballer (b. 1890)
  - Émile Colinus, French artist (b. 1884)

- James "Jabby" Jabara, American aviator, the first American jet fighter ace (b. 1923)
- November 18
    - Mike Connolly, American reporter and columnist (b. 1914)
    - Vincenzo Di Francesca, Italian Latter-Day Saint leader (b. 1888)
- November 19
    - Mendel Balberyszski, Lithuanian & Polish politician and author on the Holocaust in Lithuania (b. 1894)
    - Ted Belcher, United States Army soldier, recipient of the Medal of Honor (b. 1924)
    - Terezie Brzková, Czechoslovak film actress (b. 1875)
    - Francis Craig, American songwriter and bandleader (b. 1900)
    - Émmanuel d'Anjou, Canadian politician, member of the Canadian House of Commons (b. 1884)
    - Hens Dekkers, Dutch boxer, competed at the 1936 Olympics (b. 1915)
    - Arthur Haynes, English comedian (b. 1914)
- November 21
    - Władysław Bortnowski, Polish general in World War II (b. 1891)
    - Sir Thomas MacFarland Cherry, Australian mathematician (b. 1898)
    - Jesse Whitfield Covington, United States Navy recipient of the Medal of Honor (b. 1889)
- November 22
    - James E. Berry, American politician, four-term Lieutenant Governor of Oklahoma (b. 1881)

- Moises Frumencio da Costa Gomez, first Prime Minister of the Netherlands Antilles (b. 1907)
  - Émile Drain, French actor (b. 1890)
- November 23
  - Alvin Langdon Coburn, American photographer (b. 1882)
  - Seán T. O'Kelly, second President of Ireland (b. 1882)
- November 24
  - Ramón Amaya Amador, Honduran author (b. 1916)
  - Pat Cahill, Australian rules footballer (b. 1919)
  - Enrique Conill, Cuban sailor, competed at the 1924 Olympics (b. 1878)
- November 25
  - Fernande Albany, French actress (b. 1889)
  - Norval Baptie, Canadian speed skater, former world record holder (b. 1879)
  - Ko Cossaar, Dutch painter (b. 1874)
  - István Donogán, Hungarian discus thrower, competed in the Summer Olympic Games in 1928 and 1932 (b. 1897)
- November 26
  - Harold Burrage, American musician (b. 1931)
  - Oliver Morton Dickerson, American historian, author, and educator (b. 1875)
- November 28 – Billy Engle, Austrian-born American actor (b. 1889)

December

Walt Disney

- December 1
  - Lewis Albanese, American soldier (*Medal of Honor*) (b. 1946)
  - Peter P. Carr, Danish-born American politician, member of the Wisconsin State Senate (b. 1890)
  - Bai Chongxi, Chinese general in the National Revolutionary Army of the Republic of China (b. 1893)
  - Lewis Creber, British art director (b. 1901)
  - Ernest Daunt, Irish Anglican Archdeacon of Cork (b. 1909)
- December 2
  - Ralph Allen, Canadian journalist, editor, and novelist (b. 1913)
  - Luitzen Brouwer, Dutch mathematician and philosopher (b. 1881)
  - Giles Cooper, Anglo-Irish playwright and radio dramatist (b. 1918)
  - Conrad Wilhelm Eger, Norwegian businessman (b. 1880)
- December 4

- o Nicholas Afanasiev, Russian-French Eastern Orthodox theologian (b. 1893)
- o Thomas Carey, American-born Irish cricketer (b. 1903)
- o Crahan Denton, American actor (b. 1914)
- o Renate Ewert, German actress (b. 1933)
- December 5
  - o John Irving Bentley, American physician burned to death allegedly caused by spontaneous human combustion (b. 1874)
  - o Luciano Fernandes, Portuguese footballer (b. 1940)
- December 6
  - o Mario Alicata, Italian partisan, literary critic and politician; member of the Chamber of Deputies (b. 1918)
  - o Laurence F. Arnold, American politician, member of U.S. House of Representatives from Illinois (b. 1891)
  - o James Paul Donahue, Jr., American heir and socialite (b. 1915)
- December 8
  - o Bill Bolden, American baseball player (b. 1893)
  - o Capt. Richard Gustav Borgelin, Danish military officer (b. 1887)
  - o Maury Bray, American football player (b. 1909)
  - o Arthur Byron Coble, American mathematician (b. 1878)
- December 9
  - o Lazarus Aaronson, British poet and lecturer in economics (b. 1895)
  - o Paul G. Blazer, American oil company executive (b. 1890)

- Morris Fidanque de Castro, Governor of the United States Virgin Islands (b. 1902)
- Brian Coleman, Australian rules footballer (b. 1932)
- Pelagie Doane, American children's books illustrator (b. 1906)
- December 10 – Zoltán Baló, Hungarian general (b. 1883)
- December 11
  - Carleton Allen, Australian professor and Warden of Rhodes House, University of Oxford (b. 1887)
  - Cliff Fannin, American baseball player (b. 1924)
- December 12
  - Dino Alfieri, Italian fascist politician and envoy to the Holy See and Nazi Germany (b. 1886)
  - Nellie Briercliffe, English singer and actress (b. 1889)
  - Bill Devan, Scottish footballer (b. 1909)
- December 13
  - Jim Baker, English footballer (b. 1891)
  - Nils Frykberg, Swedish runner, competed in the 1912 Summer Olympics (b. 1888)
- December 14
  - John Atirau Asher, New Zealand tribal leader, hotelier, interpreter, racehorse owner (b. 1892)
  - Víctor Andrés Belaúnde, Peruvian diplomat, President of the General Assembly of the United Nations in 1959 (b. 1883)
  - Ronnie Byrne, Australian rules footballer (b. 1900)
  - Emma Dunn, English actress (b. 1875)
  - Verna Felton, American actress (b. 1890)
  - J. Howell Flournoy, American lawman (b. 1891)
  - Paul Galligan, Irish politician, TD (b. 1888)

- Richard Whorf, American actor (b. 1906)
- December 15
  - Major General Keith Arbuthnott, 15th Viscount of Arbuthnott, British Army officer (b. 1897)
  - Sammy Beswick, English footballer (b. 1903)
  - Walt Disney, American animated film producer and founder of The Walt Disney Company and Disneyland Resort (b. 1901)
- December 16
  - Sven Bergqvist, Swedish sportsman, International Hockey Hall of Fame inductee (b. 1914)
  - Charles Crawford Davis, American audio engineer (b. c. 1893)
  - James Verne Dusenberry, American anthropologist (b. 1906)
- December 18
  - Hon. Tara Browne, British socialite and heir to the Guinness fortune; according to some sources, he was the inspiration for the Beatles song "A Day in the Life" (b. 1945)
  - Joseph Cucchiara, Italian missionary priest (b. 1889)
- December 19 – Jack Forsyth, American football coach (b. 1892)
- December 20
  - Amram Aburbeh, Israeli rabbi; Chief Rabbi of the Sephardic congregation in Petah Tikva, Israel (b. 1894)
  - Rupert Anson, English cricketer (b. 1889)
  - Ali Asllani, Albanian poet, politician and activist (b. 1884)
  - Doc Farrell, American baseball player (b. 1901)

- December 22
  - Pádraig Ághas, Irish independent politician and schoolteacher; member of Seanad Éireann
  - Harry Beaumont, American film director (b. 1888)
  - Lucy Burns, American suffragist (b. 1879)
  - Robert Keith, American actor (b. 1898)
- December 23
  - Heimito von Doderer, Austrian Nazi author (b. 1896)
  - William Rush Dunton, founder of the American Occupational Therapy Association (b. 1868)
- December 24
  - Ernest Blackham, English footballer (b. 1898)
  - Gaspar Cassadó, Spanish cellist and composer (b. 1897)
- December 25
  - St. Elmo Brady, American academic, first African American to obtain a Ph.D. degree in chemistry in the United States (b. 1884)
  - Nick Dandolos, Greek-born American gambler (b. 1883)
- December 26
  - Ina Boudier-Bakker, Dutch novelist (b. 1875)
  - Christopher Dahl, Norwegian sailor, gold medalist at the 1924 Summer Olympics (b. 1898)
  - Noël Gallon, French composer (b. 1891)
- December 27
  - Ernest K. Bramblett, American politician, United States Congressman from California (b. 1901)
  - Ernest Burgess, Canadian-born American sociologist and academic (b. 1886)
  - Guillermo Stábile, Argentine football player and manager (b. 1905)

- December 28
  - Victor Anfuso, American politician, member of the United States House of Representatives from New York (b. 1905)
  - Frank Chodorov, American libertarian writer (b. 1887)
  - Hjalmar Christoffersen, Danish footballer, Denmark national team, silver medalist at the 1912 Summer Olympics (b. 1889)
- December 29 – Russell Brain, 1st Baron Brain, British neurologist (b. 1895)
- December 30
  - Pietro Ciriaci, Italian Cardinal of the Roman Catholic Church (b. 1885)
  - Chase A. Clark, American politician, Governor of Idaho (b. 1883)
  - Guy Earle, English cricketer (b. 1891)
  - Christian Herter, United States Secretary of State (b. 1895)
- December 31 – H. Otley Beyer, American anthropologist (b. 1883)

Nobel Prizes

- Physics – Alfred Kastler
- Chemistry – Robert S. Mulliken
- Physiology or Medicine – Peyton Rous and Charles Brenton Huggins
- Literature – Shmuel Yosef Agnon and Nelly Sachs
- Peace – not awarded

In the News

Mini skirts and bell bottoms become the fashion.

Ronnie Kray murders George Cornell in East London's Blind Beggar pub.

The Jules Rimet Trophy, the original prize for winning the FIFA World Cup, is stolen at an exhibition. It is later found by a dog named "Pickles"

The Labour Party wins the general election.

John Lennon meets Yoko Ono at the Indica Gallery.

A landslide devastates the town of Aberfan in South Wales.

The Moors Murder trial comes to a close.

Average house price £3,840.

The first £25,000 Premium Bond winner was Norman Jepson.

The Beatles play their last British live concert.

Barclaycard is launched.

Thieves steal millions of pounds worth of paintings from Dulwich Art Gallery.

www.ingramcontent.com/pod-product-compliance
Lightning Source LLC
Chambersburg PA
CBHW072137280526
45788CB00002B/682